WHY CONFORM?

a liberal studies book

COVER: Young hippy at a 'love-in' held in the grounds of Woburn Abbey, Bucks.
(*Photo by courtesy of Associated Press*)

Martyn Goff

WHY CONFORM?

a liberal studies book

HEINEMANN EDUCATIONAL BOOKS LTD
LONDON

HEINEMANN EDUCATIONAL BOOKS LTD

LONDON EDINBURGH MELBOURNE
SINGAPORE JOHANNESBURG
AUCKLAND TORONTO
HONG KONG NAIROBI
IBADAN NEW DELHI

ISBN 0 435 46538 4

Published by Heinemann Educational Books Ltd
48 Charles Street, London WIX 8AH
Printed in Great Britain by Cox & Wyman Ltd
London and Fakenham

FOR **DR. FRANK GRIMWOOD**
Warden of Moor Park College

where many of the ideas in this book
were first rehearsed with young
people – in gratitude and friendship

CONTENTS

Who, except possibly the Postmaster General, would refuse to shake hands with one of the Great Train Robbers?

– Quentin Crisp in
The Naked Civil Servant

The young always have the same problem – how to rebel and conform at the same time. They have now solved this by defying their elders and copying one another.

– ibid

1: BILKING THE BUS COMPANY

Conformity presupposes standards. Standards are moral or ethical. Our media of mass communication tend to equate 'morals' with 'sex morals'. Yet for every moral decision of a sexual nature, the average person makes twenty that are unconnected with sex. Moral standards guide us in loyalty, honesty, responsibility and trust. A single example will suffice.

If you are riding on the upper deck of a bus and the conductor accidentally misses you when collecting fares, do you call him back? Is it, after all, *his* job to collect the fare or *yours* to offer it? Does it matter? Suppose, though, that you do call him back and offer him the fare. The ride then takes you to your school, college or coffee-bar. On arrival you tell your friends how you could have got away without paying your fare; and they laugh at you. If the same situation presents itself a week later, would you again call back the conductor and offer to pay, your friends' laughter still ringing in your ears? Here we have two or three moral decisions, minor in themselves but of great symbolic importance.

A liberal studies class, to whom this example was given, emphasized two things with their answers: 1. Most of the students, who came from grammar school sixth forms, had at some time *habitually* bilked the bus or train companies. 2. Most of the students drew a line, clear to themselves, between defrauding public bodies and private people. Not one person present would have dreamt of swindling a small shopkeeper in the way they considered 'normal' when the victim was a large organization.

Whether we consciously adopt certain moral standards or feel that we are acting instinctively, the standards are there. Sixty years ago these standards would have roughly corresponded to the moral code laid down by the Established Church.

Today this code has been greatly weakened from within and without the Church. Yet we still feel that it is wrong to do this, right to do that. This book is an endeavour to find out what standards do exist, how they were evolved and how far we ought to conform to them.

THE SENSATIONAL IS NEWS

Just as our newspapers and television tend to narrow the meaning of the word 'morals' until it is synonymous with 'sex morals', so the picture of young people that they project is distorted. A student drug addict is 'news'; an aggressive, sadistic student is 'news'; a quiet or mildly fun-loving student is not. Abroad, this image of 'swinging' young English men and women is thought to include everybody. Even serious foreigners begin to believe that all our students riot, take L.S.D. or grow hair to their waists. It's not easy to convince them that such aspects apply to a tiny percentage. The majority are concerned with finding a way of life which allows them the maximum freedom to develop as individuals consistent with the same freedom for their fellows. This does not mean that we shall go so far as to avoid mentioning the more sensational aspects of non-conformity. But it is necessary to get the perspective right at the outset.

To some extent the vicar has been replaced by the psychologist, the solicitor and the doctor. All these people – and sometimes even the accountant! – are called on to listen to confessions, to advise and to distinguish between good and bad if not between right and wrong. But they do not have the great advantage of a consistent outlook and an experienced body of knowledge. Schools of psychiatry have waged fiercer wars than ever divided church from church; solicitors and doctors have very different vested interests. Not long ago there was a report in *The Times* of the annual conference of the Royal Institute of Public Health and Hygiene. One of the papers was given by Dr Richard Fox, a consultant psychiatrist. In the course of it he said: 'If two people in a wholesome relationship think they want to get married but society is postponing it for one reason or other, then good luck to them. Most of us are curious about what there is in sex, not just from one person but from different ones, and if that curiosity has to be satisfied at some time, it is better satisfied before than after marriage.'

Dr Fox is eminent and expert, but all is not as simple as that would suggest. At the end of the same debate, Dr William Burns, divisional medical officer of Antrim County Council, said: 'I would like to express my regret that the Royal Institute of Public Health and Hygiene should provide a platform for the propagation of what is known as the "new morality", that is clearly contrary to the will of God. We cannot break God's laws with impunity.'

Leaving aside Dr Burns's doubtful assumption of the role of Vicar of God in the last two sentences, we are left with the contradiction of Dr Fox's argument. Both men are qualified in the technical and more general spheres to pronounce on the subject. But if they end up diametrically opposed, how can *we* hope to distinguish between right and wrong conduct? Dr Fox's attitude may quickly lead to widespread promiscuity which in itself debases sex from a means of expressing deeply-felt love for another person to a crude physical release. Dr Burn's rule of conduct, on the other hand, only has meaning for those who are professing Christians. This at once invalidates it for a large number of people.

So that while we welcome a world in which hypocrisy plays a smaller part and convention is only followed if rational, we must not forget that the obverse of this coin is a great increase in the areas of life where we have to make our own decisions. This in itself is further complicated because in many cases our parents, once a source of authority and day-to-day wisdom, are often as confused as we are. I have heard a father berate his son for a mildly dishonest practice five minutes after proudly boasting of his own pet tax fiddle. Nor is 'if you keep on coming in after midnight, the neighbours will start talking' the way to win any rational young person's obedience and respect.

AND THEN CAME FREUD

At the turn of the century most people had a fairly good idea of what was morally acceptable or right. The Church frowned at the evil things and nodded at the good; the concept of parliamentary democracy had been firmly established; the pink (= British Empire) shaded areas on a map of the world were still increasing; and Man was still convinced that he was a logical and rational animal. Within eighteen years all those beliefs had been tumbled or damaged. If they ended by plunging the world into a war in which *ten million people* were killed, were they such a good yardstick after all? And who, after Freud's revelations, could blithely continue to talk of logical Man? New codes had to be found, tested and adopted. Half a century later we are still looking for them.

The urgency of the search is increasing. As Marshall Mcluhan has clearly shown,[1] we are entering the electronic age. More and more areas of our lives will be taken over by the machine; the cost of human labour combined with the fast-growing size of operating units makes this inevitable. Man is being simultaneously diminished and depersonalized. His only hope lies in finding ways of keeping his moral development equal to that of his technical progress.

[1] *Understanding Media*, Routledge and Sphere Books. Its theme, brilliantly adumbrated, is that the medium is the message.

THE NEED OF A MORAL CODE

In the joy of doing away with hypocritical conventions, young people have sometimes queried the need for having moral codes at all. But they are as vital to the conduct of our lives as is the highway code to the regulating of traffic. Even a bank robber fleeing from his crime will generally keep to the left, enter one-way streets from the right end and obey traffic lights. Failure to observe road rules in the main would result in complete chaos, leading to a breakdown of the whole system. Equally the abandonment of all moral codes would lead to free-for-all anarchy which only the very strong might survive.

Although belief in the Established Church has steadily declined in the last sixty years, it would be wrong to assume that its influence has deteriorated to nearly the same extent. Many of those who call themselves 'C. of E.', or even agnostics, still act as though most of the Ten Commandments guided their conduct. Nor is it necessary to be able to rattle them off. The lessons of their prohibitions and exhortations have sunk deep into our consciousness. It may have become an acceptable even an honourable thing in the course of two world wars to kill so-called enemy human beings, but Thou Shalt Not Kill is a powerful enough edict to reassert itself with great strength the moment that these emergencies are past.

In his Reith lectures Professor J. M. Carstairs said:

> Popular morality is now a wasteland, littered with the debris of broken convictions. Concepts such as honour, even honesty, have an old-fashioned sound; but nothing has taken their place.[1]

Although we may think that he is overstating the case and underestimating the force that remains in conventional Christian morality, it is interesting that a creative artist foretold this form of nihilism long before it became apparent, just as the Dadaists of 1916 had prophesied the overthrow of Victorian

[1] J. M Carstairs, *This Island Now*, Chatto & Windus.

and Edwardian values. For Julian Green, the Franco-American
novelist, wrote of W. H. Auden's poetry that

> it is characterized by complete nihilism, by contempt for every-
> thing that has been handed down by parents, that is, for the nine-
> teenth century, for the Victorian era, a rebellion against venerable
> commonplaces, against everything that has so long confined us in
> our political errors and that produced moral circumstances apt to
> hatch wars such as that of 1914 or of 1939.[1]

Green's words remind us that the state of our morals is
more than a local matter affecting one another, *important
though that may be*. For 'concepts such as honour, even honesty' affect nations as much as individuals, and grow out of
the standards of those who control the nations concerned. The
world-wide horror over Britain's behaviour at the time of
Suez was little to do with party beliefs one way or the other.
It was horror at seeing one of the last bastions of international
morality being abandoned. Hitler's pre-war attempts to justify
his territorial rapes, hypocritical though they were, show that
even thugs are aware of standards and the need to *appear* to
be conforming to them.

But first we have to evolve standards of conduct that will
allow us the maximum personal freedom commensurate with
the same degree of freedom for our parents, friends or fellow
citizens in general. Despite man's selfish lust for power or
money or sexual conquest, we must find a way of proposing
and accepting rules of living as powerful as the rules of the
road. There will still be accidents; there will still be people
who will infringe those rules. But the rules must work for the
great majority, and to do this they must be reasonable and
impartial. Once we have postulated such rules we can then
discuss individual conformity to them. For human beings
differ in many ways, not least in what they are able to contribute to society. No court ever punished a doctor for break-
ing the speed limit to reach a dying man. No court ever

[1] *Diary of Julian Green*, 1928–1957, Collins/Harvill.

convicted a driver who swerved into a 'no entry' street to save a child's life.

THE DIFFICULTIES OF BUYING A TUXEDO

Moral problems are rarely simple or uncomplicated. A few years ago I bought an evening suit at a large store where I had a charge account. It needed some alterations, so I told the assistant to charge it, go ahead with the alterations and let me know when it was ready. A week later I received a postcard asking me to collect the suit. I was served by another assistant who seemed to know all about it, I was satisfied with the alterations and I departed happily. Two months went by but no mention of the suit appeared on my monthly statements from the firm. I called at the store again, but neither of the assistants who had served me was on duty. I explained the position to a third. 'Please don't do anything about it,' he begged me. 'X will get the sack the moment they know he forgot to charge it to you.' Now morally I ought to have asked to see the buyer or manager; or returned home and written to the accounts department. And lost the young man his job? No, it's not so simple, is it?

You will note that I have just written that 'morally I ought to have asked to see the buyer'. Why 'ought'? Because *Thou Shalt Not Steal*? Because my parents brought me up to pay for what I bought whether I was asked for the money or not? Because I think it's tantamount to stealing if I obtain goods without paying for them, whether through the supplier's oversight or my own, and whether the supplier is big or small? My personal answer will become clear as you read this book. It is, however, worth adding that the reactions of older people to this story have varied widely. Some would have sent a remittance to the store anonymously; others would have given the same amount of money to a charity. Perhaps the majority would have done nothing, arguing that the responsibility to obtain payment lies with the vendor.

So we find ourselves in a world that has emerged from a set of fairly fixed standards of conduct and judgement to enter one where everything is still fluid. Just as Man has disappeared as the subject of most modern painting, so in the everyday world he is suffering from being diminished and depersonalized. To ensure that the electronic age does not get out of control, he must find a way of getting himself restored to the centre of the canvas. One of the ways of ensuring this will be to evolve a new moral code. When this exists, the need or good of conforming will be easier to see, and each man will be able to chart his progress with the least restraint needed to protect his fellows.

What are we to do until the emergence of that new code? (for life hurries on without waiting for us to conclude our moral debates). We must face life and its daily problems pragmatically. We must endeavour to remain true to ourselves even while we're respecting others. Let us try, then, to see how this might work in practice.

DISCUSSION POINTS

1. Is there really any difference between swindling a small and a large firm?

2. How far are you influenced by what your friends regard as right and wrong?

3. Do we really live in an exceptionally immoral age or is this just another of our conceits?

4. Would you report an undercharge on a bill if you knew that the assistant responsible would suffer?

2: GETTING ON WITH 'THEM'

Take any group of people, regardless of size or purpose, and a leader or leaders will emerge – or have to be appointed.[1] Rebels need co-ordinators and spokesmen; so, curiously, do anarchists. This has always been so. Even where a group has specifically disdained or tried to avoid the election of a leader, those outside the group have symbolized what it stands for by fastening on one or more pre-eminent people in it. Ninety per cent of the fuss, from both directions, over the Mick Jagger drug case[2] was not for *a* Mr Jagger, but for *the* symbol figure of a large number of young people (particularly as seen from outside this group by older, disapproving people).

All of us have to have relations with leaders throughout our lives. Some of these leaders are automatic, like our parents; others almost automatic, like our head teachers, college principals and school or college captains. Still others are partly chosen, like bosses (you may decide not to join a particular firm because you take an instant dislike to the managing director at your first interview); or M.P.s, though here your one vote will do little to defeat the man you dislike. Finally there are those you choose, in small organizations that you join, either in the deliberate sense of nominating and lobbying for a particular person; or by shunning a drama group or tennis club because you can't stand its president or secretary.

In all these cases we have, sometimes painfully, to become aware of the standards laid down by the leaders. Once we have learnt their rules, we tend to evaluate them: that's sensible, that's nonsense. Finally we decide, consciously or subconsciously how far we are going to conform. Can we change

[1] William's Golding's novel *Lord of the Flies*, Faber, contains an excellent description of how this happens.

[2] Summer 1967. He was convicted but later successfully appealed against his sentence.

the bits we don't like? Or just disregard them? Every group needs some organization and a certain number of ideas, however simple. Having accepted this, are we prepared to compromise with *existing* demands to make the life of the group reasonably smooth? Let's take the main areas of authority with which we are almost bound to come into contact and see how this works in practice.

MY FATHER, RIGHT OR WRONG

Our first relations with authority are with our parents. During our early years they feed, clothe and protect us, and in return demand our obedience. Even a unit as small as the family must have someone in charge if there is not to be chaos. To start with, tiny children cannot fend for themselves. Later, too, someone must decide what is going to be eaten, who is going to buy and cook it, and when it will be consumed. As well as making it possible for a group of people to live in a box (= house or flat), this demand for obedience accustoms us to the inevitable demands that authority will make right through our lives. Not even a Prime Minister can disobey the laws of his country. A charge against Mr Wilson for exceeding the speed limit *might* be waived under certain circumstances; one for uttering a forged cheque could never be.

Now all this sounds fine and logical in theory. Practice has a way of introducing extraordinary complications. When a father says to his fifteen-year-old daughter, 'you must be home by 10.30 p.m.', he is simply exercising his reasonable authority as a father. But when the daughter replies that *all* her friends are allowed out until midnight, that she'll look stupid and childish having to leave the party an hour and a half early, and that anyway what difference does it make to him when she comes in, father's authority no longer seems reasonable. He can then take the attitude of divine authority: till twenty-one you're my responsibility and you'll obey my orders. Or he can apply the protective attitude: 'Whatever your friends' fathers allow, I know too many cases of girls going astray by being out late at your age.' Lastly he can justify his negative for the benefit of the whole group: 'by coming in that late, you'll wake me, your mother and your little brothers and sisters.'

But this hardly touches on the further complications that attend so simple a decision in everyday life. One fifteen-year-old daughter may be mentally and emotionally the equivalent of the average eighteen-year-old; another may be young for her age. Yet again, one girl may be associating with friends whom her parents regard as respectable and trustworthy; another may have joined a coffee-bar crew whose very appearance fills the father and mother with horror. Nor is that all. In one case there may be a history of rebellion and disobedience turning this one evening into the proverbial straw that breaks the camel's back; in another it may be the first time that the girl has ever questioned a parental decision of this sort.

Now we are all aware that biologically the parents conceive and give birth to the child, then feed and protect it until it is old enough to 'fly off' on its own. Equally we know that human parents at least tend to delay this day, partly by being over-fearful for the child, partly by wanting to retain the child's company for their selfish pleasures. So what is really at stake is the timing of the transfer of power from parent to child. This differs in different societies – it's younger at the moment in America than in England, older in Italy than both – and in different ages. The tendency since the Second World War is for young people to gain their independence at progressively lower ages. This has made relations between parent and child more difficult, not, as one might have supposed at first sight, the reverse.

When the parent is in absolute and recognized control, life tends to be smooth, however frustrating it may be for the growing child. If mother says 'Get your hair cut!', the order is carried out. But once the child will only accept orders that it deems reasonable, huge areas of argument are opened up. If the parents try to be strict, they are laughed at or met with the final ultimatum: 'I'll leave home.' If they are permissive, they suffer from the feeling that they are harming the child by spoiling him or her; while the child has been known to complain that he has nothing to rebel against!

Why has there been a general breakdown, or at least a lessening in, parental authority? Partly because children mature more quickly both physically and mentally; better feeding and health standards, exposure to television and other media of communication that do not discriminate between ages have all helped the process. Partly because talk and knowledge of psychiatry has combined with the lowered prestige of Church and State to undermine parents' belief in themselves. To be a good leader you must believe you are qualified for the job. God tended to support this qualification for every parent until the end of the first decade of this century. Since then too few parents have operated under His aegis for this feeling to have the same strength. Similarly, if you keep on telling fathers and mother that all their urges and decisions are sex-inspired (Freud) or power-inspired (Adler), the conflict with *their* inherited ideas of divine parental authority seriously undermines the latter. Parallel with this, and therefore speeding its movements, young people have acquired greater power through having more money to spend and through being given greater say in family decisions, leading to a total increase in their status at the very moment that their parents' has diminished.

But beyond a certain point, struggles between the generations can only do harm. Mankind has still to find a better protective envelope from which to emerge than the family, and current in-fighting can only weaken this unit further. During the last hundred years young people have probably had too little to say in the running of the unit, but opting out or fighting it now will only replace frustration with chaos. If parents will take the trouble to define their own positions, then the edicts or requests they pronounce from those positions will have the force of logic. Few of us are going to conform to an order to be in by 10.30 p.m. if it's issued under the banner of: 'Because I say so, that's why.' Equally, few will – or certainly should – resist a fairly stated reason: 'Because it wakes your mother and she can't get back to sleep.' The more smoothly a family unit runs, the more pleasant life is for each member of it. Obedience to rational requests and demands is a necessity. Responsibility for ensuring that the demands are reasonable and the obedience reasonably precise are divided between the two parties.

HEAD TEACHERS AS DICTATORS

Teachers and head teachers, on the other hand, have not in the main derived *their* authority from the Church, at least during the last hundred years. Except for Church schools and so-called Public Schools, it is the State that is the responsible body. Young people may be more cynical about the State than their opposite numbers fifty and hundred years ago, but they have not yet seriously started to challenge its authority. All the same, head teachers are not as autocratic as they might have been in 1900 or 1850. Three things have contributed to this:

1. They no longer have the same certainty of being backed up by the parents. Recent years have seen a tendency for parents to defy school authority when it counters their own permissive attitudes.
2. Younger teachers, themselves only fresh from being rebellious or nonconforming teenagers, no longer give head teachers the automatic awe and respect that was once general.

3. A widespread tendency to debunk those in positions of power, prestige or fame is part of the age we live in. A headmaster's progress along a crowded corridor in 1968 is much less fearful and impressive than it was in 1938: after all, he eats, sleeps and goes to the lavatory just like us!

Having outlined the diminution of power, it is only fair to add that a great deal still remains. A head teacher of any strength will affect the staff and through them the students, so that one man or woman can still impress his or her ideas and outlook on a thousand or fifteen hundred young people. And because of the numbers involved, because there isn't the tension that automatically arises from the closeness of mother to son or daughter to father, rough conformity to a good head teacher's edicts is fairly general. It rarely leads to much need for compromise, and it makes the passage through school years more pleasant and smooth.

TO SIR, NEUTRALLY

Teachers, though, bring back some of the difficulties of parental relationships because they are much nearer to the pupil. Once again there is a tendency to conform just sufficiently to avoid making life unpleasant for oneself and one's friends. Of course there are a minority of young people who go through their school lives at odds with all authority. On the whole, though, it is a period of life which for the majority provides less friction than almost any other set of relationships they will have. Authority is clearly derived, clearly defined and mainly disinterested. No one would pretend that teachers are even reasonably paid. Many of them teach from a sense of vocation. The comparative success in obtaining the conformity of young people in the lower reaches of education shows what is possible where certain elementary precepts are the bases of the teacher-pupil relationship.

Age has something to do with it. However sharply defined and clearly disinterested the authority, attitudes towards it do begin to vary and become less acquiescent as the later teens are approached. The need to assert oneself, to prove to oneself as well as to others that one is an independent human being leads to a more brash and defiant attitude towards authority. The defiance may take the form of unauthorized or outlandish clothing and hair styles; or of open though minor disobedience. Boys particularly reach a stage of brinkmanship with their cheekiness. We are back in the area of delicate balance: too much conformity may mean lack of proper development and spirit; too little makes the school difficult to run, or even tense and unhappy. To be truly independent we have to surrender some of our liberty; it's asking rather a lot to expect a sixteen- or seventeen-year-old to judge just how much.

SACRIFICING FREEDOM TO GET IT

In the opening chapter of this book we saw how we would all find ourselves living in a state of chaos unless we had moral standards to guide us. We compared a set of rules defining these standards with the rules that govern our behaviour on the roads. The same analogy will serve to show us the relationship between a surrender of liberty and the attainment of independence. If everyone may do exactly what they like, then we have no protection against being robbed or attacked: our freedom is illusory. As soon as we sacrifice some of that freedom by agreeing to obey laws not to attack, rob or kill people, our freedom is greatly increased. In short, it's the same as the chaos that would supervene on the roads if we didn't start out by giving up our freedom to drive as fast as we like where we like.

The trouble starts when we try to lay down what rules and how many of them. In the family unit this is difficult, as we saw in the case of the father and his fifteen-year-old daughter: they had different ideas of what limits were needed to protect their own freedom and independence. In the case of the school the rules are unilaterally imposed by the man or woman qualified to judge how to give the maximum freedom to the maximum number consistent with minimal harm to everyone else. In the relationship that most people have with their employers there is a new complication: the supply and demand of labour.

OUT TO WORK

The law of the land compels you to go to school until you are fifteen. Necessity, in the form of the need to earn money to feed, house and clothe yourself, drives you to work. But whereas most people have little choice in the school they go to, there is more choice when it comes to work. This choice depends on our qualifications and abilities, it is true; but it also depends on the state of the labour market. Where there is widespread unemployment, for example, choice is narrow and the employer's power only restricted by the various (increasing) welfare Acts of Parliament. Where there are more jobs than applicants for them, the employer's chance of obtaining conformity to absurd or excessively strict rules is unlikely.

There are other complications affecting our behaviour to employers. One of these is ambition. If we want to get on in a firm or organization of any sort we must be prepared to conform not only to its rules but also to its outlook. At twenty I was shocked when an R.A.F. Group Captain, who sat frequently on interviewing boards for potential officers, said to me: 'There's only one question I ask – and from myself – "would I like that bloke sitting next to me in the Mess?"' I still think it was a morally outrageous way of judging people, but I have learnt that it is a canon of selection that is widely practised.

Conformity to further our ambitions points to an oft re-

curring struggle between what we know to be right and what
we know will make our lives more pleasant. If the boss asks
us to do something which is *legally* honest but morally against
our principles, what do we do? Supposing we are sent to repair a television set, only to find that the fault was a loose wire
to the wall plug. Our time and journey may have been worth
7s. 6d., but we are told to hand over a bill that states: 'To
locating and rectifying fault in receiver – £1 5s. od.' The
charge is legal but excessive. But to argue with the boss or
warn the customer may put an end to our chances of becoming
the next works foreman. Do we conform to our knowledge
of what is right (where right equals a fair price for the job);
or do we accept that the man responsible for laying down the
charges knows best? Indeed, couldn't it even be that over the
whole range of small repair jobs he only makes a fair profit
by averaging out the amounts charged, so that bigger profits
are made on the simpler jobs?

FRIEND BEFORE COUNTRY

This conflict between our feeling of what is right or wrong
and authority's view of the same subject extends to one of the
ultimate authorities, the State itself. 'Our country!' wrote A. S.
Mackenzie at the beginning of the nineteenth century. 'In her
intercourse with foreign nations, may she always be in the
right; but our country, right our wrong.'

For a hundred years after this few people would have quar-
relled with its sentiments. Yet by 1940 E. M. Forster, one of
the most distinguished of twentieth-century novelists, was
able to say: 'I hate the idea of causes, and if I had to choose between betraying my country and betraying my friend, I hope
I should have the guts to betray my country.' The bravery
– or foolhardiness, depending on how you look at it – of making such a statement is greatly enhanced when we learn that
it was made on the radio soon after the start of the Second

World War. Its distance in moral stance from Mackenzie shows how far attitudes had changed in less than a century and a half. The need to reassess our relation to any authority with whom we are connected is constant. In the case of the family the simple fact of growing older ensures that this will happen; elsewhere we have to try to assess the changes in ourselves and others. Otherwise we end by acting from bases that have long ago lost their validity.

Whatever the authority, however, there are certain basic conditions that we are right to demand before submitting to its moral authority. These are:

1. Confident leadership;
2. Clearly stated reasons for the demands and curbs laid on us;
3. Reasonable rewards for obeying them;
4. Good, non-hypocritical example set by the authority.

We have already considered 1 and 2 at length. 3 recognizes that the restraints imposed on us are neither easy nor natural. If the complexity of modern society requires ever-increasing surrender of our own selfish needs and desires, we ought to be given the bonus of appreciation. Yet parents, for example, are quick to praise their children – *to other parents*. Employers tend to accept the outstanding as the normal, and grumble at the rest. Authority ought always to be ready to mark its acknowledgement of the effort made to conform to its rules by concessions and praise on its side.

Finally, while we may deplore the debunking of those among us touched by creative magic – great artists, authors, singers, mathematicians, and the like – pricking the bubble of over-privileged leadership has made the world a slightly better place to live in. Total equality is a myth; men are too various in every way for that. But the assumption of privileged ways of conduct because of a title or office in itself is also passing. The corollary of this is that those in power must be *seen* to be obeying the rules they lay down for others. Only then will the call to conform have the ring of truth.

DISCUSSION POINTS

1. At what age should our parents cease to have absolute authority over us?
2. Do we prefer those in authority over us to be strong and, if necessary, severe as long as they are fair?
3. Is the conflict between the generations really any greater now than it used to be?
4. Can we be rebels and yet succeed in modern industry?
5. Do we agree with E. M. Forster – or A. S. Mackenzie?

3: DOWN WITH SKOOL!

In the last chapter we briefly considered our relations to those in authority in schools. Now we turn to the whole field of education. This includes not only our attitudes to teachers, but also to what is taught, to how it is taught and to what obligations such teaching and learning places on us. The law of the land and the absence of any alternative system means that we all have to go through the existing educational system. Yet there is much in it with which some of us disagree, and our attitudes to this will affect our outlook and possibly our future.

A few years ago Paul Chambers, then chairman of I.C.I., one of the largest companies in England, complained that honours graduates joining his company were often ill-equipped to deal with their seniors, their equals and their juniors. It is in fact possible to go right through a grammar school and university education almost entirely on the strength of written brilliance. Yet in everyday life the ability to get on with other people, to be given orders by them or to give them orders, is of paramount importance in all cases save those of a few experts. The know-how of many jobs can be learnt in a matter of weeks or months; the human relationships connected with them need constant adjustment and readjustment throughout its span.

With the present educational system somewhat weighted in favour of the boy or girl who is good at expressing his or her thoughts and learning on paper, those without this ability but with strong personalities may feel at a great disadvantage. While the latter may be the very people who could successfully hold down executive positions requiring the handling of personnel, the initial rebuff deters them from trying. This in turn leads to their rejecting some or all of the system, and marking this rejection by a refusal to conform. Here it is not so much a question of being right or wrong in refusing to follow the rules, as not having any other ways of expressing dissatisfaction with a system that denies the fulfilment of personality.

We might have hoped that this situation would improve now that education itself has become a subject of deep and widespread study, accompanied by new methods and experiments in teaching. But on the other side of the scales we are seeing a constant increase in the importance of qualifications. More and more jobs are open to graduates only, while the competition for university places – and so for 'A' levels – becomes the aim of the first twelve or thirteen years of schooling. This in turn lessens the time that can be spent on more general education: learning to enjoy the arts, working out attitudes to religion, sex, politics; in short considering the matter of this book! And doing this not in the sense of a quick read, but slowly enough to allow plenty of time for digestion and discussion. The person whose whole bent is towards the narrow study of a few subjects, and the subsequent expression of that knowledge through pen and paper, has little difficulty in conforming to the current educational structure. The rest either can't or won't, or just pretend to.

Conformity despite a deep-seated apprehension that all is far from well makes life smoother at the time, but it can also be the seed of lifelong frustration. A boy may find that, despite an engaging manner that makes him popular among his equals and teachers, he always does badly in written exams. While inwardly becoming aware that his particular personality and abilities don't fit the present system, he continues to conform without protest. Gradually he begins to accept second and third place in every way, often ending up with a job that exploits a quarter of his true ability to deal with human beings. By this time he has lost sight of the original reason for his frustration. He only feels, and frequently goes on feeling, that somewhere life has cheated him.

Another boy in the same situation may apprehend that it is the rigid system that is at fault. So he begins to kick against it, gradually becoming labelled as a rebel or even a trouble-maker. It would be rash to suggest that in a majority of cases the second young man will do better in life. He may, for he could well become a professional rebel: a militant union leader, chairman of a vociferous minority group, a radical politician and so on. What is likely, though, is that he will be a less frustrated person than his conforming opposite number. Where a system fails to allow us to develop fully, the fault may lie in its rigidity – or in us. To protect ourselves we may have to protest. All that society can reasonably ask is that we do it within a democratic, non-aggressive, non-criminal frame-work.

MONEY OR KNOWLEDGE

The boy or girl who is at odds with the current educational set-up may not be all that common; the one who is torn be-tween the desire to gain more education and the pressure to earn a living is more frequently met. Here, too, there are still class differences, though these are happily lessening. While fewer working-class parents are likely to dissuade their children from going on to any form of higher education than was common even a few years ago, it is still true that such parents will rarely try to persuade the doubtful child to stay on at school. Middle-class parents, on the other hand, are inclined to go to the other extreme. Even where a child has been positively hostile to everything in the educational system, attempts are made to force it to have another shot.

How far should we conform to our parents' wishes in de-ciding whether to go further in education; and, which is part and parcel of the same decision, what sort of career to adopt? Fortunately this is a less pressing question than it used to be. Slowly but surely parents have come to accept that a son or daughter should do what he or she wants to in life; and that such guidance as is required comes better from qualified careers advisers and psychologists. But pressures do continue to exist, and sometimes are more subtly applied than they used to be.

Although much parental pressure either to leave school as soon as possible or to go in for a specific, safe career is better disregarded, this is far from a total truth. We mostly have to learn our lessons from personal experience for them to affect us fully, but parents can sometimes save us from pitfalls. They can also advise us badly from good motives. The father who tries to persuade his unsuitable son to join the family business to protect the long-term interest of the mother and, perhaps, of the younger children, is certainly being somewhat altruistic. Yet conformity to our own abilities and leanings remains in most cases the safest guide.

WHAT OUR FRIENDS THINK

Apart from the parents who want us to leave school and the parents who urge us to stay on, there are other pressures from those of our own age. And as parental influence has declined, at least in this sphere, particularly during the last ten years, so has that of our friends and others of our own age increased. This influence may be explicit or implicit. A boy may decide to go to a Technical or Further Education College on leaving school: specialized qualification or further 'O' levels may seem important before moving into the commercial world. But if his friends immediately obtain well-paid jobs, he is going to need a strong character not to be swayed from his long-term aim by the difference between his purchasing power and theirs. Sometimes, fortunately, the person concerned will make new friends who are roughly in the same position. Otherwise his inability to *conform* to the spending habits of his friends can soon make a young man's life very frustrating. Once more we see that conformity is not only a vertically imposed pattern. It can be horizontal as well.

At seventeen or eighteen years of age it may be hard enough

to settle down to another three, five or even seven years of study to attain a first-class position and commensurate salary. To have to do this while one's friends have cars, a liberal supply of new clothes and, if a boy the wherewithal to give girls a good time, can impose an extra burden that can make the first minor academic failure an excuse to drop out altogether. It is easy for older people to cite the huge difference in pay between the successful graduate and the unskilled worker when both reach their mid-thirties. To the man in his late teens the disparity *at that moment* is far more tantalizing.

DROP-OUTS

'What a waste!' people will say when someone does drop out of higher education, either through simple academic failure or through outside pressures such as those we have described. It is, too, and one that both country and individual can ill afford. We are still far from being able to satisfy the demand for all forms of higher education. The boys or girls who drop out half-way are not only wasting the specialized education that has been given them, but have also been filling places that could have been filled by others who might have stayed the course. If society is to give the individual the greatest opportunity, he or she must be prepared to make every reasonable effort to use that opportunity to the full. No one expects a boy to go on with a course for which he finds himself manifestly unsuited after some months; but where, as in the case of accepting the chance for higher education, conformity is the equivalent of fulfilling a contract, it should only be abandoned as a last resort.

Sometimes people want to give up a course not because they are unsuited for it, but because the world of education, with its particular disciplines, becomes too much for them. Earlier maturity, the lessening of the Church as a moral force and the diminution of parental authority have made young people more sceptical of institutional discipline. The uniform of a college scarf or tie is fast being replaced by the national, often international, uniform of long hair, narrow levis or whatever happens to be the fad of the moment. Discipline as a force needed by nearly everybody is discounted as a thing in itself. Each rule must be capable of logical argument; otherwise conformity is out.

Such a vague shot at anarchy is probably bad both for the individual and the institution. If it has appeared to work over the last few years, it is because there was a lot of dead wood that needed cutting away; and because the reserve of authority in most institutions, particularly universities and old-established colleges, was sufficient to withstand some crumbling at the outer edges. It is a central theme of this book that a mass of human beings can only live together, in a college, town or country, under a framework of clearly described rules. These rules must always be a delicate balance between freedom and conformity. Unless the individual learns this while he or she is receiving the more academic side of education, society will be threatened by chaos in its day to day running. The same is true of the college if students demand a degree of freedom from conformity that goes beyond the point where the rules guarantee a necessary degree of order.

Nothing that I have stated so far is meant to exclude the extension of democracy, above all in the fields of higher education. To make the college library a place where everyone can work in peace may mean the imposition of a rigid rule of silence, to be enforced if necessary by penalty. But this is quite different from allowing the students to have representatives on the library committee who are responsible for deciding on the books to be bought, the hours of opening and the general services the library is to provide. These two areas of authority are frequently confused. Where freedom for all can only be achieved by discipline, this must be imposed from above and conformity ensured by threat of punishment. Where

c

convenience and use can be gained most effectively by representational, elected government combining with authority, the struggle to achieve this is legitimate.

DRESS – OPTIONAL

If, then, we propose to obtain the advantage of further education, we must be prepared to conform to the minimum conditions required to make its operation effective for the greatest number. This can be made easier by the authority in question dispensing with unnecessary rules. Quiet, minimum attendances, reasonable exam results are necessary for an institution's efficient functioning. Compulsory physical training, attendance at a religious assembly or a veto on cars *may* not be. On both sides the issues are fairly straightforward. Other rules are not. How far should students have complete right to dress as they like? At first glance it might not seem to make any difference if a few of them turn up at college in swimming trunks or topless dresses. But, of course, it does: both would interfere with the maintaining of reasonable discipline. Then what about jeans or shoulder-length hair (for boys) or necklaces made of bells (for girls)? As in censorship in the theatre, such lines are difficult to draw. We can only fall back on the greatest freedom that doesn't compromise the degree of order needed to let the college function efficiently.

In our present set-up in most of the Western world, basic education is provided as a duty by the State and accepted as a duty by the child. Higher education is still a privilege. Almost no privileges in life come unencumbered by a price, rules or duties. If human nature were ideal, we would expect people to observe this without any pressure. As it isn't, the necessary conformity can only be obtained from *everybody* by being enforced, with penalties if needed. That the most educated have sometimes become the least disciplined during the last few years is a surprising and unfortunate development.

DISCUSSION POINTS

1. Should written qualifications like university degrees, be a condition of entering into most top jobs?
2. How far should one listen to one's friends when deciding on a career?
3. Should we persist with a course of study despite initial failure?
4. Should school uniforms be compulsory?

5: LIVING ON TICK

The incident of the evening dress in the introductory chapter tells us something of the changing attitude to money. Fifty years ago the country was divided into three economic tiers:

1. The huge working class whose only concern was to earn enough to keep body and soul together;
2. The large middle class whose guiding principles were the maintenance of visible standards coupled with the value of thrift;
3. The upper classes, whose wealth was largely inherited and/or in land and who were comparatively casual and cavalier towards it.

Nobody in class 1 could possibly have had a charge account; most people in class 2 would have frowned at the idea of one; and nearly all those in class 3 would have *assumed* their right to credit wherever they shopped. To this day the landed aristocracy and the new millionaires are the slowest payers!

In many ways the attitudes of the second class were the most important, partly because once the working class rose above the subsistence level they tended to aspire to them; and partly because the upper classes were numerically of little consequence. Crowning these attitudes was the cliché about saving for a rainy day. However respectably you yourself behaved, there were still acts of God: storms, wars, illness were the threats, and a healthy bank balance the only partial defence against them. The National Health Service, pensions for everyone and (almost) full employment were still idealists' visions. If you earned £10 a week, then £7 was the maximum you should spend. Nor must we underestimate the dying force of this attitude fifty years later: it is one of the major differences between parents and children of the fifties and sixties.

In the years leading up to the Second World War, and for a while after it, middle-class parents wanted to place their

children in *secure* jobs. For the brainy and apt this might mean
the law, medicine or accountancy. For the rest, who were of
course the majority, it usually meant banking, insurance, the
armed forces and the lower ranks of the civil service. Because
of the security these jobs brought, and the aura of respecta-
bility that unthinkingly surrounds them, the two qualities
became mixed in the minds of many people. Even if a
shop had been able to offer the same security in the form
of pension, holidays and other benefits, the middle-class parent
would have turned his thumbs down. Shops were not
'respectable'.[1]

It would be an exaggeration to add that these same parents
never considered whether the given job in a bank or insurance
company also satisfied and fulfilled their children. Even apti-
tude was comparatively unimportant. But in most cases re-
spectability and security were the guiding middle-class lights
in job-seeking. In the working classes it was simply a matter
of leaving school as soon as possible and getting a job, any
job. Male children might follow in their father's footsteps,
but only because the paths were known and easier to approach.
For different but parallel reasons the middle-class boy whose
father had his own business tended to join that father once
his education was completed.

Finally we must mention that a comparatively small number
of people went in for higher education. These were drawn
almost entirely from classes 2 and 3 (the working-class boy
who obtained his degree by scholarships alone was a rare pheno-
menon); and while the universities did have minimal entrance
standards, they were indeed minimal: the ability to pay was
much more important. As a complement to this, degrees were
necessary over a much narrower range of jobs than is the case

[1] In the last ten years I have been faced with parents refusing to allow
their sons to work for me in a bookshop except as brief holiday jobs
commensurate with navvying (!), because the retails trades are not yet
quite 'respectable'.

today. They were not necessarily the main, or only, reason for going to a university in the first place.

SECURE JOBS – AND DULL, TOO

The advent of various forms of *national* welfare and employment security in the last decade has greatly lessened the attraction of job security *in the eyes of young people*. At the same time a gradual lessening of parental authority had aided this movement so that many girls and boys now opt for careers which run counter to their parents' approval. Here we have an outstanding example of a widespread failure to conform to standards laid down by an older generation. Unfortunately, though, other pressures have somewhat vitiated this advantage.

With considerably higher wages (compared to the cost of living) and more generous amounts of pocket money, the post-war world has seen a very rapid growth of teenage spending; and the advent of skilled marketing techniques to exploit it. Where a working-class boy or girl of the thirties might never have had a *new* item of clothing, having always to make do with an older brother's or sister's cast-off's, a whole new segment of the clothing industry now exists to persuade them of the absolute need to keep abreast of fashion. The cut of a boy's collar or the length of a girl's skirt has become as compulsory as a Judge's wig! Nor are middle-class children left untouched by this change. Instead of the thrice-annual visit to the 'safe' department store with mother, they, too, must keep up with the Nigels and Amandas.

I have cited clothes, but similar pressures apply to gramophone records, cosmetics, holidays and, above all, to motorcars. Almost every boy *expects* to have a car or motorcycle as soon as he is old enough to obtain a driving licence. Working-class boys are often content to share a car with two or three others; their middle-class counterparts may receive some form of parental subsidy in buying or running the car. But an over-whelming percentage of the young male population of this country *wants* a vehicle of some sort.

So while young people can today resist parental pressure to opt primarily for security, they find it much more difficult to resist the pressures of fashion from their own peers. Money dominates their lives as strongly as ever it did that of a Victorian industrialist, and they are inevitably drawn to jobs that are highly paid from day one. A driver's mate on a long-distance lorry might easily earn fifteen pounds a week from the start. It is almost impossible to make him realize, in the full sense of that word, that he will be earning very little more in ten years' time. The call of the clothes shop and car showroom is too great. What is even more sad is that so many of the most interesting and rewarding jobs – teaching, nursing, librarian-ship for example – are among the lowest paid when the degree of responsibility and knowledge are taken into account. Equally, jobs requiring long, poorly paid apprenticeships seem very unattractive to people constantly bombarded by advertisements telling them of all the things they *must* buy.

BUY, BUY, BUY!

It is difficult to over-emphasize the force of the pressures deployed on young people to persuade them to part with their money. Open advertising campaigns are only one of the many ways in which business attacks the appetites and vanity of the young person. The constant statement in television plays, for example, that it is *normal* for every youngster to have some sort of vehicle waiting at the gate soon persuades anyone without one that he or she is *sub*-normal. Nor is it easy for us to assess the economic sense and nonsense (both are there!) of hire purchase if every advert for it shows users to be wise as well as swinging – a young, very attractive middle-class couple with a *sensible* house and a *sensible* car. One stands in front of

the other, while the handsome husband, posed with a pair of
serious-looking spectacles *in his hand*, smiles at his sexy but not
silly wife.

Many youngsters are convinced that they resist advertising
and so remain untouched by the pressures to earn money
quickly. Alternatively they attribute the worst of advertising
to small get-rich-quick firms. But it was one of our most
famous oil companies that put out a particularly insidious ad
a few years ago. Beside a picture of a young, attractive mum,
framed by her two slightly constipated-looking children, were
the words: IS THERE A CONNECTION BETWEEN THE G.C.E.
AND OIL-FIRED CENTRAL HEATING? (Mrs 1970 thinks you
may owe it to your children to get warmth through —— Ltd).
How many mums had conscious or subconscious doubts about
how far they were undermining their children by depriving
them of proper warmth conducive to laying 'O' levels like
eggs! And how many children in semi-heated houses were
given another excuse for their failures? If giant oil companies
can stoop to this form of pressure, we can begin to guess what
lesser organizations might try.

BUY NOW, PAY LATER

And if the pressure is great on the teenager, it becomes even
more relentless on the young married couple. Hundreds of
advertisements are designed to nudge them into having things
that they can only afford through hire purchase. H.P. itself
has become respectable, partly because it has clearly succeeded
in projecting itself as such; partly because the moment the
majority of people use or do something, it tends to become
morally acceptable. (The skilful projection is shown by the
very name of one of the most famous of the H.P. companies:
Lombard Banking. Most people have a vague idea that Lombard Street is the City of London's centre, and the word
'Banking' has a noble, solid sound.) Younger people tend to

equate H.P. with house mortgage: both enable you to possess something before you have saved for it. But the older generation of our class 2, the middle classes, would not agree with this; and the young couples giving in to commercial pressures to secure things they cannot yet afford are *morally* wrong in their parents' eyes. Let us look at this a little more closely.

We obtain a mortgage, or loan, on a house by putting down a deposit and paying off the remainder over a period like twenty years. We also pay interest on the money so 'borrowed', but only on the actual sum annually outstanding. With hire purchase we also put down a deposit on the thing we are buying and pay off the balance in instalments (we literally 'hire' the thing until they are all paid), but we usually have to pay interest on the initial sum 'borrowed' until the last penny is paid. This means that hire-purchase costs much more interest than a mortgage, though not in itself sufficient to warrant the older generation's condemnation. Their real sense of moral outrage centres on the difference in the object itself. Most things bought on H.P. are expendable: cars, motorcycles, refrigerators, record players, transistor radios and even furniture tend to last for a small number of years. Houses, on the other hand, outlast most people's lifetimes; and normally *increase* in value meanwhile (the seemingly endless rise of building costs and the price of undeveloped land assure this).

Now although the more old-fashioned members of the older generation may tend to become a little self-righteous in the face of H.P., it is important for us to know where we stand in relation to it. For H.P. is the key to a whole new concept of life summed up by the phrase, *Live Now – Pay Later* (compare the airlines' adverts: *Fly Now – Pay Later*). It may have been wrong to buy something on tick in 1932 when one's job was daily threatened by the slump. Is it still wrong now, when we have (almost) full employment and myriad social security and insurance schemes to protect us against temporary set-backs? Our parents, many of them with memories

of the thirties, of unemployment and bankruptcies, would say
'yes'; and this affirmation would be even more forceful where
young married families are concerned. It might be fair to add
that there was, in their attitudes, a touch of the puritan, too:
it is healthier not to have the luxuries of life too quickly or
easily. Early possession leads people to becoming blasé and
having *less* to look forward to.

As with so many things, it is the disapprovers who worry
most about the rightness of a particular action. We have begun
to accept hire purchase as a *normal* part of our lives. It may be,
but it remains important to realize that we are operating a
moral choice every time we put our signature on the bottom
line of an H.P. agreement. In exactly the same way most of us
want a health service, police force and educational system but
are only willing to contribute a certain amount of the necessary
taxes towards them. Above that amount (not always nor often
worked out consciously) we tend to move into the same blur-
red moral world as that in which we embrace the advantages
of H.P.: we want something on the cheap.

ON THE FIRM

There are many ways in which we try to achieve this; most
of them would have been considered immoral if not illegal
by our parents. Working-class men become house painters or
gardeners on Sunday as long as they are paid in cash which
does not have to be declared to the Inland Revenue. Middle-
class men will charge things 'to the firm' that they should pay
for out of their own pockets. Expense-account meals which are
really for friends; or cars paid for by the firm which are almost
exclusively used for private purposes are two obvious cases.
Expensive personal phone calls are made from the office;
personal letters and parcels are posted there; sundry purchases
are made from petty cash (one bar of soap for washroom and
three to take home!). This sort of trivial pecuniary advantage

has probably been taken throughout history. But the huge increase in personal taxes has given people what they have come to consider a 'moral' right to practise this form of dishonesty!

Our attitudes to taxation, economically central to our lives, are very complicated. I purposely described tax fiddling as a 'form of dishonesty' because it is; but unfortunately governments themselves tend to blur the edges of the judgement. On a number of occasions in the last twenty years Chancellors of the Exchequer have introduced into their budgets measures designed to close (legal) tax loopholes. They have done this with an air of – 'there, that's got you!' – leaving accountants and tax advisers to search for other related loopholes. Gradually the whole thing has developed into a battle between the Treasury and the more cunning type of accountants. Now most of these struggles relate to the closing of formerly *legal* gaps in the tax laws. But such is human nature that the ethos in which this is done suggests to many people that the whole area of tax paying is a battleground between the citizen and the Tax Inspector. Tax evasion becomes both a game and, at worst, an amoral approach on the citizen's part. Not surprisingly he resents the use of adjectives like dishonest to describe what he is doing.

Money is the means by which we pay for the necessities and luxuries in our lives. Money is also the roughest of guides to our merits as workers and thinkers (cf. the commissionaire at the Dorchester Hotel, London, who is reputed to earn more than a university professor). Being constantly bombarded by visual and written messages to persuade us of our inadequacy if we are without a thousand and one contemporary products, our need for money grows as fast as it is fed. This leads to lowered standards of personal honesty, particularly in relation to payment of taxes, and the glamorizing of highly paid jobs whatever their suitability or non-monetary reward. Our moral attitudes are further complicated because more and more people believe that unrestricted capitalism is not necessarily a good

way of life. Having lost belief in the overall system, they find
it harder to obey its more trivial rules. If A's firm exploits the
needs of the emergent countries by making and selling them
arms and ammunition, how can it be a moral offence to take
home and use the firm's drawing-pins?

DISCUSSION POINTS

1. How important are salaries in the choice of a career?

2. Do you believe that advertisers influence you to spend
more than you would, for instance, in the Soviet Union (where
there is far less advertising)?

3. Ought you to have some financial security (= money
saved) before you get married?

4. Is using the firm's phone without paying for the calls
really dishonest?

5: TO SEX – OR NOT TO SEX

At the beginning of this book I made it clear that the field of morality, and so of conformity, was very wide, while many people thought of it only in the context of sex. I must now balance that by adding that everything connected with the sexual act does seem to strike at and from very deep roots. A boy may get excited or obdurate about his parents' constant requests to get his hair cut.[1] But this irritation may be mild compared to the show of prejudice when a sexual taboo is broken. No amount of reference to anthropological studies showing that a dozen different uncivilized tribes practised a dozen different and conflicting sexual practices will sway the prejudiced. What they believe to be right is, to them, *natural*.

Our subconscious plays a considerable part across the whole range of our actions and reactions. Because we tend to repress the majority of our sexual desires, our subconscious fears and wishes in this department are very powerful. Where taboos have been inherited, or deeply instilled at an early age, we will fight the slightest sign of them with particular vigour. For example, if we find a man ranting and roaring against flagellation as part of the sexual act, the chances are that he is fighting a subconscious desire for it in himself. A Home Secretary, who was virulently anti-homosexual while in office, was actually arrested for homosexual practices after his retirement from public life!

These, though, are sexual prejudices affecting minorities. The area where we encounter the most heated discussion and feeling is that of pre-marital sex. And this affects almost everyone. Biologically, the human being reaches the height of his

[1] Charles Berg in *The Unconscious Significance of Hair*, Allen & Unwin, suggests that the cutting of hair has a sexual significance both for the male child and for the parents.

sexual power between middle and late teens. Socially, Western society has endeavoured to postpone sexual intercourse until marriage; or, failing that, at least until the early twenties. This had (notice the past tense!) excellent reasoning behind it. Only a family unit can offer the child the love and security it needs. Birth control has been too vague and difficult to obtain to rule out unwanted children. In those circumstances young people were wisely discouraged from the commission of an act that could lead to yet more illegitimate children.

To assist society in discouraging the act two aids were invoked. The first was the dangers of venereal disease. Syphilis, and to a lesser extent gonorrhoea, were nasty and could have serious consequences. The cure was also disagreeable until the discovery of penicillin reduced VD to the ranks of other unpleasant germs. They might be easily caught but they were also easily cured: no teenager brimful of sex was going to be put off by that any longer.

SEX OR LOVE

The second aid was more vague. Sex without love, young people were told, was empty, mechanical, unsatisfying. There was something in this, but expressed in that way without qualification, it was patently untrue. Besides, what is love? History abounds with those who fell in love at first sight and remained married for a lifetime. Would intercourse on that first night have fulfilled that condition? If not, at what stage does love that doesn't qualify for sex become love that does?

There are good reasons why boys (for whom the problem is usually greater) and girls should postpone sexual intercourse until marriage or at least maturity. But the case for this must be stated logically and without hypocrisy. It must be seen to be free from the taint of denying the young merely because the middle-aged were denied it when they were young. And it must be recognized that conformity will still be beyond the power of some individuals. It is nonsense to pretend that we are all equally highly sexed or that sublimating sex into other channels like the arts or social work comes as easily to everyone.

So the current situation is that a ban on pre-marital intercourse can no longer be justified by the risk of producing illegitimate children – *in theory*. In practice use of the pill, or other prophylactic methods, is not yet nearly wide enough. But the force of this will decline as methods of birth control become more easily available to everybody. Venereal diseases are still with us but their easier cure makes them a small deterrent to the drives that lead us to promiscuity. Finally, sex without love is as difficult to pin down as love is to define. And yet . . .

The dilemma is once more that few are willing to believe without personal experience; while the degree of personal experience required takes one beyond the point of no return. To put this into simple terms is to state that promiscuity *does* debase sex to a purely physical experience of rapidly decreasing satisfaction. By the time, though, that we have proved this for ourselves, it is too late to return to a state of innocence. Love is easy to arouse in others and as easily aroused in oneself for someone else. To sustain it is far more difficult. The sexual act is one of the chief ways in which the human being achieves this. Since our society is still based on marriage or long-term unions, we cannot afford to debase the principal means of upholding such unions, at least in their early years (later all kinds of interdependencies help: father/daughter roles; mother/son roles; the need for particular sorts of companionships; a sense of balance that fulfils personality; and so on).

THE PRICE IS HIGH

We can't *prove* the truth of this, though if older people were more honest and forthright about their sexual experience, expectations and disappointments, we might come near to it.

Mother warning daughter in a vague way about the dangers of sexual promiscuity is unlikely to achieve much. A dozen middle-aged women doing the same thing and citing unsensational but saddening experience conceivably might. Such warnings must be accompanied by the honest admission that sex *is* fun, and that in the early stages it provides exciting and interesting experiences. The bill to be met later is for something experienced. Many people would not, however, be prepared to pay the price if they could be convinced of its almost inevitable coming.

This debasing of the sexual act through over-promiscuous pre-marital experience may damage not only the *quality* of sex relations with one's lifetime partner; the promiscuity in itself can easily become a habit that cannot be broken. There are married people who are not shattered when one or other of the partners goes to bed with someone else. These are few, human nature being what it is; and we shall never know what pangs of jealousy they suffer. For most married people the other partner's infidelity is very painful; and it remains one of the principal reasons for marriage breakdowns and divorce.

Here we ought to note that we can no longer go on talking in the plural, for the partners to a love or marital relationship are not equal in every way. Leaving out the inevitable exceptions, most women *feel* more deeply than men. A brief love-affair, carelessly ended, may leave the man with a bitter-sweet memory; the girl is often deeply shattered or disturbed. The force of all the arguments against pre-marital or extra-marital intercourse apply more strongly to girls for this reason.

GOING TO THE DOGS

This consideration of current and near-future attitudes to pre-marital sex and extra-marital sex touches on a view of contemporary morality that extends over many of the fields we are considering: the decline of morality. When people talk of a steep moral decline they usually mean that attitudes to sex are more permissive – and less good. The possibility, though, is that these are less hypocritical and *more* responsible. It is not only more honest for us to consider whether promiscuous sex debases the act for the future than to mumble about 'wrong' or 'evil', venereal diseases or (emotively) unwanted children. It is surely more responsible. As human beings we have the power to do a great many things – to make, for example, an aeroplane. Rather than ban the manufacture of planes because they can be used for war, isn't it *more* responsible to produce them, then try to ensure that they are only put to peaceful purposes? Man's progress in civilization can be marked as much by his control over himself as by his technological invention. When he is finally relieved of the anxiety of bringing unwanted children into the world by the universal distribution of the birth pill, his restraint in controlling his sexual drive will be an *advance* in civilization. The sexual revolution of the last few years has set us on a gentle climb rather than the often pictured and highly colourful slope to some modern hell.

This is underlined if we consider our attitudes to sexual deviation and nonconformity. We have just seen the passing of a law that permits adult male homosexuals the same freedom in private as we have always allowed heterosexuals. The position before this enactment, though, was not something reaching back into distant history. It dated only from 1885. In early Greek times homosexuality was looked upon indulgently. In the last two thousand years different countries and periods have adopted all the different shades of opinion that lie between Greek times and 1885. Ethical values of all sorts show few gradual evolutions in Man's history. Unlikely as it may seem to us at this moment, another period of puritan reaction is far from impossible.

Once we admit that a sexual deviation is not a wilfully

diabolic act but something resulting from psychological or physiological disturbance, we must tolerate it in the kindest sense of that word. Naturally we must protect children and others not strong or old enough to protect themselves. But we have no more right to expect conformity from the sexual lame than we have to demand sporting conformity from the physically lame. Society must protect itself and its members. Neither are harmed by what two lesbians do in private.

KINKIER THAN THOU

Homosexuality and lesbianism are fairly clear cut. Deviation within the normal sexual field is harder to define. Most of us have some sadistic or masochistic strains in our sexual make-up. Mild, controlled indulgence of these can lead to greater sexual pleasure. Marriage is long and the human being can become sexually bored with one partner. As Desmond Morris says:

> As an inventive species it should be natural for us to experiment with any posture we like – the more the better, in fact, because this will increase sexual novelty, and prevent sexual boredom between members of a long-mated pair.[1]

But when mild sadism turns into inflicting serious pain and ends by *replacing* the normal sex act, our nonconformity has gone too far and becomes dangerous. It is no longer enough to throw up our hands in mock (or real) horror at every sexual act that goes beyond the simplest form. On the other hand we cannot expect society to approve variations that physically or mentally harm another person – or ourselves.

In the distinction I am trying to make, it is easier to understand the point beyond which we may harm another person. To bite someone playfully in the course of the sexual act may be mutually gratifying and harmless; to whip them may still

[1] Desmond Morris, *The Naked Ape*, Jonathan Cape, 1967.

be superficially gratifying, though harmful at least to the victim. But when it comes to harming ourselves, we think we are the only judges. If it gives us pleasure to be hurt, then we have the right to encourage a willing person to inflict pain on us. But it is not that simple. Society has helped to rear and educate us, has invested in us and is entitled to a return. If we damage ourselves mentally or physically, we are depriving it of its rights.

DISCUSSION POINTS

1. If we accept in theory that promiscuous sexual activity debases the act itself, how are we to limit ourselves in practice now that venereal diseases and unwanted children can be more easily cured or checked?

2. If love ought to precede sex how can we discriminate between it and simple physical desire?

3. Has Man morally declined more in the last few years then previously, or is this an illusion created by endless newspaper introspection?

4. Is a puritan reaction likely in face of the present permissiveness?

6: IS GOD LOVE?

If everything to do with sex touches deep roots, as I have already suggested, then anything pertaining to religion seems to affect sensitive ones. For many years it was even considered bad taste to discuss religion in some middle-class circles. Only, perhaps, during the last few years, when the Church has begun to question itself *publicly* from within[1] has this attitude changed. Even now most of us feel differently about dropping a Bible to dropping any other book; and few of us would shout in a church even when there was no one present whose susceptibilities might be offended. Just as we are morally still living on Christianity's deposit account, so the aura of the Church invests even the most agnostic of us.

The tacit ban on discussing religion in middle-class circles almost certainly stemmed from uncertainty. The fervent believer has never been afraid to argue his case; on the contrary, he has usually been delighted to have the chance of attempting some proselytization. The English middle classes, on the other hand, continued to operate behind a façade of religiosity while true belief became comparatively rare. Churchgoing has declined enormously in the twentieth century, but even among those who go every Sunday there are some who do it to set an example to their children; others for whom the ritual is so deeply implanted that they cannot willingly give it up; and yet others who treat the visits as social occasions. They meet their friends and neighbours as they might at a pub or community hall; they see and are seen.

It is easy to make fun of this or label it hypocritical, but such reactions are themselves superficial. Man has an innate need 'to believe in something'; and this need also appears to demand that the something is impressive (full of ritual) and group inspired. Even where belief in the central faith of the religion has

[1] As, for example, in the controversial book by the Bishop of Woolwich, J. A. T. Robinson, *Honest to God*, S.C.M.

been weakened, the form surrounding it can continue to fulfil some of the need. If this were not so all-powerful, the differing claims made by the world's major religions to be the One Truth would long ago have destroyed them all. Christian man or Moslem man has not maintained his belief despite the other out of a childish obstinacy, but because his need to believe is so overriding.

DOES THE CHURCH BELIEVE IN GOD?

Since this need is a continuing one, why is there a rapidly growing nonconformity where the Church is concerned? Many young people in particular say that they believe in God or at least would like to, but that they find the Church as an organization outmoded, hollow and smug. This would appear to conflict with the idea that older people derive some satisfaction from the *forms* of worship in themselves. Both parties in fact want to believe but only the older can draw satisfactorily on the Church's balance. The younger are too conscious of the ambivalence in the Church's actions.

'Thou shalt not kill.' The Commandment is explicit, absolutely unambiguous and not hedged with a single qualification. There is nothing about it being all right to kill if you're attacked first; if your land and property is being attacked; or if you are convinced that your opponent is evil. Yet British troops about to go into battle to kill Germans were blessed by bishops and lesser fry. Nor has the Church condemned the atom or hydrogen bombs ceaselessly and unequivocally. This being the case, say many young people, how can we do otherwise than opt out of Christianity altogether? Its ritual is hypocritical; its outlook opportunist.

The sad thing is that there is much truth in this; *and* that we still need some kind of Church, whether it's Christian, Moslem, Hindu or Jewish.

> At first sight, it is surprising that religion has been so successful, but
> its extreme potency is simply a measure of the strength of our
> fundamental biological tendency, inherited directly from our mon-
> key and ape ancestors, to submit ourselves to an all-powerful,
> dominant member of the group . . . . Only a common belief will
> cement us together and keep us under control.[1]

The trouble is that we want to see signs of rapid change in
our religious organizations, whereas such things take generations. The establishment of a few coffee-bars in parish church
crypts hardly scratches at the sort of changes required. A
complete re-tooling is necessary, and this may take decades.

However disturbing it is to have to accept the claims of a
dozen major religions that each one alone is the Truth, it
becomes totally discouraging to find endless splinter groups
within the main camps, each protecting its particular slant on
the religion as fiercely as any nationalist defends his frontiers.
Here again an ecumenical wave is slowly beginning to flow
through many of the factions, but the complexity of the
organizations involved, not to mention the dominance in
each of old men, can only mean that current teenagers will have
grandchildren before a great deal can be achieved.

If we agree that most of us do need something to believe
in, then it is not enough to criticize the Church and stand waiting for a substitute to appear. The Church already has vast
experience in ministering to this basic need. It will probably
continue to be the answer for a large number of people. The
size of this number, though, will depend on the ability of
the Church to change, not in superficial ways, but seriously
and deeply. It will have to face up to its attitude to war, poverty
and its own feudal hierarchy. It may have to go to the people,
in the sense of worker priests, rather than wait for the people
to come to it. Priests are only men, but they will still have to
be *seen* trying to live an exemplary life if they are to win the
confidence of far more cynical and knowing congregations

[1] Desmond Morris, *The Naked Ape*, Cape, 1967.

than any they have had to deal with during the last two
thousand years.

SEVENTH-DAY HEDONISTS

Even if we assume that the Church can successfully remodel
its image to become (or remain) a force in the lives of many,
there will be another whole segment of the population for
whom it can have no meaning; and this group often includes
the more literate and articulate members of society. At present these people are expected to behave with awe and re-
verence to the Church. So Sunday behaviour is still limited by
the Church's restraints. Theatres may not be opened, though
this would surely be the best of all days for hard-working
people to visit them. School assemblies continue to be based
on the fiction that all the pupils are practising Christians. The
Services have compulsory church parades (could there be a
more paradoxical piece of hypocrisy than that?). The BBC
devotes a fraction of the time to agnostics and atheists that it
gives to the Church. All these things harm the Church for that
part of the population who are non-believers.

What I have just said is roughly true of many countries,
but precisely so of England, for here the Church is *established* by
the State. Some people think that the Church will never begin
to recover until it is disestablished. Certainly it is better for a
religious organization to be divorced from politics. Those of
us who look to the Church for guidance do so for help in
spiritual matters. We are not encouraged when we find the
Church concerning itself with temporal things like the abdica-
tion of kings or the support of war aims.

The criticisms that I have made or implied of the Church
as an organization must not be taken too far. We cannot heap
on the current Church the sins of Popes or Archbishops of past
centuries. We cannot expect the Church to divest itself of its
considerable wealth and property. As long as its ritual is centred

on a house of God, so long will it need considerable funds to maintain such places. It is easy to fall in to the error of asking how the Church can blithely possess so much wealth while so many of its parishioners are poor. But if we concede that these same poor are as much in need of spiritual as of material sustenance, then we must allow that the Church needs large funds to carry out its duties.

THIS WORLD, OR THE NEXT

Most of the comments we have so far made about the Church could be applied to the majority of the world's major religions. But one of the key points of religious faith does divide those religions into two groups. This is the belief in after-life. The Christian Churches specifically believe in this and have always used it as carrot and threat. 'We know your lot is hard. but hold on and be good; a wonderful life in the next world will be yours.' Or – 'If you get drunk, commit adultery and tell lies in this world, you'll get a pretty lowly position in the next one.' Millions of peasants throughout history have been sustained by one or the other, or a mixture of both.

It is absurd to be dogmatic about an after-life. Nobody knows *for certain* and no one is ever likely to know until it is too late! If it seems unlikely or impossible, then so would the idea of pictures travelling through walls, mountains and forests to the inhabitants of eighteenth-century England. For us TV is a commonplace. What we can rightly demand is the withdrawal of both carrot and threat. The possibility of Heaven for the immaterial bits of us is not sufficient reason for allowing starvation, slums and cruelty. Our lives here on earth are precious, and each one is equally precious, whatever our brains or beauty, inheritance or nationality. We must aim at a situation where every human being has a chance to develop to the limit of his or her ability. If there is an after-life that is a bonus, not a welfare compensation.

Equally we must expect people to give of their best for their own sakes and society's, not because hellfire and brimstone are waiting for them in the next world if their standards lapse. Every time we have a few days of fine weather, someone will say: 'You see: we'll have to pay for this. Tomorrow it'll be raining.' This quasi-moral approach to meteorology is pretty odd, but extended to life as a whole it can be positively dangerous. Historically it may have been useful for the Church to control the merging masses by uttering threats about hell. Currently it is using a weapon as anachronistic as a brougham would be for crossing Europe.

A WORLD FOR CAREFUL DRIVERS ONLY

If after-life is a major bone of contention between believer and agnostic, then Injustice with a capital 'I' is a close-runner. How can a baby of one year be guilty of anything? And if that's so, then what heavenly justice can there be for such a child to be burnt, maimed or diseased to a point of extreme suffering? If God is good, wise, loving, how can He allow such things, let alone permit wars, floods, famines? If, on the other hand, He cannot control such things, how could He ever have created the world or the universe?

It is possible to build a machine – a plane or a car – and then not be able to control what it does in certain circumstances or with others at the wheel. 'There is the car', the manufacturer may say, 'it's up to you to use it how you will, preferably, of course, for good but possibly for bad'. If we accept this view of God's relation to the world, then the reward for good and punishment for bad becomes even stranger. Once we admit that God has no control over the world He created, then He is in no position to hand out praise or criticism of those who compose it. Such a basic conception of God can make little appeal to modern man.

If we conceive of God as a moral force, a spirit or a Being,

who brought order from chaos, who appears to each of us
in the guise of our conscience or soul, we are getting nearer
a modern conception of the heart of religion. The trouble here
is that such a God's chief function is the laying-down of a
moral code of living. But unless we believe the Christian or
Moslem or other religious myth, we know that this moral code
can only have been evolved by God's representatives on earth.
And they, whatever their titles or offices, are human beings
and subject to all the whims and passions of human nature.
Unless an act of faith helps us to believe that they are indeed
people with a special vision or spirit which qualifies them to
guide the peoples of the world.

Since the world today is divided into those who have this
faith and those who lack it, we are poised at a tricky point in
Man's development. It would be silly to fall into the error of
pretending that Man hasn't gone through a dozen similar
crises in his development. But three factors magnify the problem for us:

1. The total population of the world was so much smaller
   in the past;
2. The pace of life and technical evolution was fractionally
   as fast as it has been in the twentieth century;
3. Man was never as intellectually self-conscious as he is
   today.

It is difficult enough for the Church to evolve a modern moral
code for those we term its believers. So many of its former
moral strictures have been outdated by twentieth-century de-
velopments. It is equally difficult for the body of non-believers
to evolve a code, for here leadership is replaced by vague terms
like conscience or intangible ones like tolerance and sympathy.
But most difficult of all is that these two codes must somehow
coexist. So far during the Christian era both parties (the
Church's adherents formed the majority) followed or at least
paid lip-service to Christian morality. The chances of this

continuing are small. The resolution of this problem is one of the biggest tasks facing twentieth-century man. All the technological invention in the world will be useless unless he can control it – and himself.

DISCUSSION POINTS

1. Are there good reasons for going to Church even if we can no longer accept the total Christian myth?

2. Should all Sunday restrictions inspired by the Church apply to non-believers as well? Doesn't it harm the Church if they do?

3. Would the Church be more acceptable in the twentieth century if it divested itself of much of its wealth and show?

4. Should promise of another world influence our actions in this one?

7: MY CAR IS LONGER THAN YOURS

'Keeping up with the Joneses' is a catch-phrase at which we all laugh – then consciously or unconsciously try to do just that. We may no longer worry much about upsetting the vicar or the local squire; we are very concerned about the impressions we make on our friends, neighbours and social equals. A favourite posh Sunday paper advert of the last few years shows a handsome young couple looking out of the window of a model terrace house. Below, and next door, are a slightly more handsome couple with their sports car or small, second car or jet-propelled lawn-mower. The 'you, too, could own a . . .' caption is almost unnecessary.

Advertisers long ago discovered that one of the easiest ways to tempt people to buy their wares was to imply that everyone else was already doing so. Recent years have seen an extra turn of this screw by the care taken by commercial interests to foster these changes of fashion. Hardly has one style become the latest thing than the next is introduced. Where those affected by changing styles in, for example, dress or furnishing were once mainly the leisured classes, cheapness, consequent on mass production, has widened fashion's influence to almost everyone. Here, in an area where conformity may eventually lead to mediocre uniformity, there are fewest rebels.

At middle-aged, middle-class levels, keeping up with the Joneses is tempered by streaks of individuality and the limits of the pocket. If the pressure is for a fridge *and* a certain standard of car *and* central heating, there will always be some people in the road who can't afford them. With young people the fashionable items are comparatively cheap and within reach of most: clothes, cosmetics, hairstyles and L.Ps. Conformity has reached surprisingly high percentages among students and young workers alike. It might pay us to see why this is so.

I have already stated that the young of recent years give short shrift to much that was hypocritical in the standards of their elders. They are cynical about politicians, patriots and priests. Whereas their opposite numbers thirty years ago wanted nothing better than to grow up quickly, today's young continue to play the teenager well beyond their teens. But life is too complicated and difficult to be waged by each person individually, so they join horizontally with those of their own age. These peer groups are the new authority; and conformity lies with *their* standards instead of with the old vertical ones.

This loss of belief in authority, as we have already seen, comes as the aftermath of twenty years in which authority was seen to have failed. Freud, having undermined Man's belief that he was a rational animal, was followed by two ghastly world wars. If the standards of the Victorian Age were right – Church, Democratic State, Progress, Empire – how did it all end in the totally unnecessary murder of 10,000,000 people? The latest, post-Second World War generation were not to be duped again. They would seek leaders from the uncorrupted among themselves.

All this was happening while a new phase in the industrial revolution was taking place: mass production, assisted by the rapid discovery of synthetic materials, was increasing at a huge rate. In the early part of the century a rich man might have had his silk shirts cut and made in Jermyn Street. Today a top couturier designs shirts for a mass producer who then makes them cheaply in a synthetic material. However 'exclusive' the design, 100,000 men can be wearing the shirt a week after it has been launched. Given mass production and horizontal fashion pressures, it's only a short while before a given shirt can be seen from one end of the country to another. A further design, another launching campaign in the national Press and on the box, and its successor becomes equally widespread.

Now mass production in the case of shirts is being echoed in every way, in retailing as well as manufacturing. The

trend, in short, is to massive combines producing for super-
markets. Since the new basis of commerce is quantity, firms
merge, stores get larger and choice grows smaller. The larger
the unit, the greater the efficiency, we are told, though what
is meant is the greater the profitability.[1] From this follows
the greatest quantities of the smallest numbers. If a store sells
10,000 pots of marmalade each week, it could drive the hardest
bargain and make the largest profit if it could persuade all its
customers to buy the same brand. In practice it will still offer
some choice, though this will be much less than what was
offered by the little grocer around the corner. The tendency
to conformity through fashion is thus supported by current
commercial trends.

At first sight this might seem wholly bad. Taste is a dangerous subject since many of us think that our taste is good
while everyone else's is bad. But taste informed by knowledge
and experience can be improved. For many years good taste
was laid down by the aristocracy partly because they had the
time to acquire it. There may be a certain amount of esoteric
nonsense connected with wines, but most of us would agree
that there are good and bad wines. We also know that we can
learn or be taught to distinguish between the two. But today
taste in clothes, furnishings and cars is largely laid down by the
makers of these goods.[2] And they, of course, will always have
to bear profitability in mind. (Critics of these things are little
more than manufacturer's publicists. When have we heard
a motoring correspondent start his review with the words:
'This is a thoroughly bad car, ugly, poorly designed and unlikely to last'? Yes these words are commonplace for theatre,
book or art reviews.)

[1] Like all large-scale generalizations, this one has exceptions: Marks
& Spencer's, for example, are a splendid example of efficiency and profitability combined.

[2] For a full explanation of why this is so, we must turn to J. K.
Galbraith's *The New Industrial State*, Hamish Hamilton.

The slight alleviation of this grim picture, where profit and corporation ethics rule all, comes from the area of design which is steadily improving everywhere. Manufacturers have become design conscious; public bodies like the Fine Arts Commission or the Design Centre exist to encourage good design. We may all end up wearing the identical shirt as we drive the identical car, but at least both will be designed for their respective purposes. This is not, though, enough.

LET'S ALL LOOK ALIKE

If a note of dissent has been sounded throughout this chapter, it's not because the profit motive is necessarily bad or evil; even monopolies and mergers may have their good points if a greater number of people can enjoy the good things of life. But material satisfaction is not sufficient. When we all start to talk, eat and dress absolutely alike, a great deal of the colour will have gone out of our daily lives; and this colour makes life so much more interesting and varied. Here, then, we see the real danger of conformity to fashions dictated by commercial interests: they lead almost inevitably to uniformity and drabness.

If we agree that the present trend is undesirable, what can we do about it? There may be fifty unknown pop-groups as good as the Kinks, but merit is only one of the factors that will move fans to ask for a particular record. In the same way, when the fashion designers have decreed that this year's colour is sludge green, the widest ranges and best stock supplies will be found in that colour. In both cases newspapers and magazine features, constant publicity, exciting window-dressing and radio and television exposure will condition us to ask for the Kinks and sludge green. To hope that thousands will stand up and say: 'Enough! We want the new record by the Konks and bashful pink shirts' is wishful thinking. What we can and must do is to educate people to a point where they will regard the 'fashionable' as cynically as they now treat the political.

GOOD-BYE TO BEING FRANK

Fashion pressures don't stop at sludge green and a new pop-group. They extend through the *necessity* of having a car radio or dish-washing machine to modes of speech and manners. Once upon a time friends ended telephone conversations with 'so long'; then it was 'cheerio'; followed in its turn by 'bye-bye'. Currently it's something that sounds like 'Buy-eee', almost whispered in a casual, throwaway manner on a falling fifth. Although most of these greetings are lazy or soft, this is not very important. It only becomes so when it extends to other fields. Jacques Barzun sums this up in this passage[1]:

> Thus in the common round of committee meetings, it is necessary to differ, but also impossible. Manners therefore decree that one shall say: 'I may be all wrong, but –'; 'You'll correct me if I'm wrong'; 'I'm only thinking aloud'; 'It's only a crazy notion that crossed my mind.' The lexicon of pussyfooting is familiar. On its title page should appear the motto: 'Never say "I think", which is obsolete; always say "I feel", as in "I feel that the Treasurer has been dipping into the till"; then if you are wrong, you haven't said anything.' Though the shuffling vocabulary is all hypocrisy, it is routine hypocrisy concealing a desperate wish to placate. Torn between the fear of error and the fear of being thought inhuman, hating to be misunderstood and hating even worse to be misliked, we verbally cast off self-confidence and throw ourselves on the mercy of the court, saying 'frankly' before every sentence and giving warning when we are going to be 'candid'.

It is difficult to avoid these habits, so widespread have they

[1] Jacques Barzun, *The House of Intellect*, Secker & Warburg and Mercury Books.

become. They start by being symptoms of mental laziness or evasion; they are often caught by others in parrot fashion (a dominating speaker in a small group saying 'you know' at the end of each sentence will be aped by two or three of that group before an hour's out, though it was not one of their verbal habits before that hour). Other forms of manners are equally catching, and in most cases as welcome as slipshod verbal habits are unwelcome.

ON BEST BEHAVIOUR

Manners, in the sense of politeness and consideration, need only be questioned when they become excessive. Most people would agree that an able-bodied man should give up his seat in a train or bus to an old woman. Fewer people would applaud the same treatment of any woman: 'if they want equal pay and opportunity, they can't expect deferential treatment as well' would be the opposition's view. Some middle- and upper-class people still stand up when a woman comes into the room. We might state that the first example is necessary good manners, the second preferable, and the last charming. But if a woman entering the room is a hostess preparing a meal, and so going backwards and forwards to the kitchen, then it would be *excessive* if the men stood up each time she came in.

In rejecting certain values and standards laid down by older generations, younger people have been guilty of carelessly excluding much that was valuable. Good manners, shorn of the falsity and specious gentility sometimes associated with that term, are to human society as oil is to a car engine. In London people queue for buses, first come first in, and the weak, small or otherwise handicapped get equal treatment with the strong, big and brawny. In Rome there is no such fairness, and the invariable scrums and struggles result in injuries and inequitability. It *may* be excessive to have to remember to say the woman's name first in a mixed introduction, but a formal introduction of some sort does make subsequent conversation easier. It *may* not matter whether the men at a table wait for the women before starting on the food; it does that people talk with full mouths: it's ugly to have to stare at an open mouth of half-masticated food. Even the basic 'please' and 'thank you' can transform an order given or carried out into a pleasure.

Etiquette should change with the times, but conformity to the new or amended manners does make life more pleasant for all. It may at first glance seem an anachronism for men to walk on the outside along street pavements. But this piece of gallantry has a simple logic: the outside person is the more likely to get splashed by passing traffic. Man is better protected for this with his trousers than woman with her silk stockings. On the other hand it may now be *safer* for a woman to open the offside passenger car door in a busy street for herself than for two people to be standing in the road causing a larger, and perhaps longer, obstruction.

POMP AND SECURITY

Many of Man's actions have a symbolic as well as an actual meaning, the former often enshrined in ritual. In common with other animals we need this ritual to increase our sense of security. Marriage is still a major event in our society. By a contract between two people, who may not even know each other very well, an undertaking is given that they will do their best to spend the whole of the rest of their lives together. The more ritual in which we can envelop this contract, the more we can impress on them the seriousness of the step they are taking. So we have the simple physical action of the man slipping a ring on the girl's finger. But this ring is also a constant symbol, for the wife, of the contract she has entered into. (As men and women grow more equal, we may well see more and more couples *exchanging* rings on this occasion.)

It is easy to scoff at a religious ceremony, or at tails for the men and elaborate gowns for the women. Each of these rituals, however, increases the sense of occasion for all concerned. Conformity to such habits is not a weak-kneed giving-in to outmoded forms, but a realization that Man has a strong biological need to hedge his security with myths and symbols. It's as easy to stand outside and laugh at this as it is for the non-golfer to be amused by two men hitting a ball round a course, according to a whole set of rules, then following it. To the golfer his hits and walks have a meaning. So for the bride and 'groom have the bells and confetti.

Although there is a definite distinction between ritual and manners at a wedding, the two do overlap. Something that starts out as one may carry on as the other, and vice versa. This is true, too, of a third ingredient. Keeping to the same example, marriage, we find that social customs also vary, horizontally, with the class of those getting married. Top hats and tails will only apply to upper and upper middle-class levels, or for those aspiring to such levels. Even within this class, attendance at certain snob churches will give the marriage an extra cachet. And conformity to the horizontal pressures of this kind, when we move from the special case of the wedding to some more general situations, can be almost wholly bad. Of all such situations those involving alcohol and tobacco are the most prevalent, though other drugs are beginning to have some importance.

NONE FOR THE ROAD

Our attitudes to drinking alcohol are compounded of absurd puritanism and great indulgence. By the use of the word 'absurd' I am not necessarily implying that alcohol is a good thing. Although considered a stimulant, it is in fact a depressant; in even mild excess it may cause people to behave aggressively or savagely; and it is a major contributory cause to a wide variety of accidents. But to restrict its use by having 'licensing laws' is a farce, as is the licensing of certain restaurants but not others. For these restrictions are counterbalanced by a giant industry, tremendous advertising campaigns and a large source of government revenue. My concern is not, however, with the rights, wrongs and follies of this situation but with the resulting social mores.

The first and most important is the virtual pillorying of the teetotaller. So extensively have our business and social lives been constructed round alcohol that it becomes difficult to live them and refuse it. This is made more so because the others at a business lunch or private cocktail party actively *resent* the abstainer. He is, in saying, 'no, thank you', adversely criticizing the drinkers – or so they consciously or subconsciously feel. And they will make every endeavour to break down his refusal to conform. It can easily reach a stage where he is known as a 'bad sport' or 'killjoy', while his social, and even business, rating is downgraded. To refuse to conform in the face of this type of campaign can be quite a trial; many confess defeat by appearing to give in, standing or sitting through whole parties or lunches clutching the same hardly touched glass. It's a sad comment that a habit that is not one of man's biological needs has become so seemingly natural that it takes courage to reject it.

Like many other drugs from aspirins to opium, alcohol can *seem* to be a necessity. 'I can't unwind at the end of a day's work until I've had a couple of whiskies.' If this was not strictly true to start with, it can quickly become so through psychological accustoming. The social position of alcohol will do the rest. People begin to find it difficult to meet and talk except over a drink. If protest is made that alcohol is bad for the liver or stomach, the answer comes pat: 'I know, I know, but I have to choose between that and nervous troubles – and without whisky I'd be a wreck in no time – so I'll settle for cirrhosis of the liver.'

Most parties are geared to alcohol; nearly all business lunches are threaded with it. We celebrate by drinking; commiserate by drinking. We cling to a whole hocus–pocus of misinformation about alcohol and its effects; and we venerate our dependence on it. In the face of this it is increasingly difficult to refuse to conform to what is certainly neither necessary nor beneficial.

TWENTY CANCERS A DAY

If the chief pressures for drinking come from friends and acquaintances, those for smoking come from advertisements. The sole exception to this, and an important one, is in early teenage years. At thirteen or fourteen the non-smoking members of a group or gang feel less masculine or grown-up if they resist the example of the smokers. At later ages their social groups exert almost no pressure to persuade them to smoke, nor is the non-smoker criticizing the smoker by his abstention. Here the rapidly growing propaganda about the connections between tobacco and lung cancer, and nicotine and other bronchial troubles, is helping the non-smoker to keep free of the pressures brought to bear on the non-drinker. The need to conform to the smoking habit can therefore be correlated with the weakness of the individual in the face of the barrage of cigarette manufacturer's advertising. Once more the position is immorally complicated by the government being a major beneficiary from the smoker. As long as alcohol and tobacco are large producers of revenue it will be difficult to get their potential medical harm into focus.

GOING TO POT

With both these drugs the addicts rely on an attitude that admits some harm but pretends that greater suffering would follow abstinence. When we come to narcotics a different and more emotional climate reigns on both sides. The antis see drugs, particularly *hard* drugs, as something that could undermine and perhaps destroy society as we know it. The pros claim that *soft* narcotics are actually less harmful than tobacco or alcohol. Both tend to be dogmatic in a field where comparatively little research has so far been carried out.

Basically all drugs, from tranquillizers to heroin, are bad in the sense that they only provide temporary escape from a given situation; and that by the nature of their effect on the human system they are required in ever-increasing doses to remain effective. To encourage or persuade people to start on them is criminal because to the best of our medical knowledge the *normal* person has no need of them, and the mildly neurotic are only encouraged to avert their attention from their real problems. We *may* one day be able to prove that marijuana, for example, is a pleasant way of heightening our enjoyment of certain pleasures without any side-effects. Until that day, to conform to the habit of smoking it merely because it is fashionable among people with whom we associate, must surely be stupid and may even be criminal in more than the legal sense.

The hidden and obvious pressures to conform to everything that is currently fashionable are very powerful. They threaten to form our taste for us and to leave us with a sense of being deprived if we resist or cannot afford them. We can only resist these pressures by consciously and continually acknowledging that they exist, and are dangerous.

DISCUSSION POINTS

1. How far should we actively resist commercially inspired fashion?
2. Do good manners matter?
3. Is alcohol a necessity for smooth social life?
4. Why do we go on bothering with the form and ceremony of marriage when so many marriages go on the rocks?

8: ART FOR YOUR SAKE

When we discussed marriage in Chapter 7 I hinted at the importance of symbols and myths. Most of our inherited race and society culture comes down to us in the form of myths that almost every major civilization in the world seems to have created at one time or another, often simultaneously. So simple and straightforward a myth as the Don Juan story reappears in history in various guises often enough for us to say that Man needed such a legend. The drawing of animals on the walls of prehistoric caves would appear to fulfil another need: young people of today paste cut-out photos of pop stars on their bedroom walls.

These myths and symbols have been enshrined in what we now call the Arts. The attitudes of different people to the Arts of their countries and races can tell us a great deal about their social and moral habits. Given that the Moslem religion forbids the making of human images in painting and sculpture, we would be likely to guess that their women would be almost totally hidden by their clothes, their men not much less. The interaction of symbol – or forbidden symbol – and art goes further. The brilliant filigree work to be seen on Moroccan palaces and mosques is due to the same narrowing of the artists' and craftsmen's fields. Prevented from depicting human beings, they could give all their attention to the most intricate pattern-making.

In the Christian era the artist has emerged through two major phases. In the first he was a servant, at one time of the Church, at another of Royalty and finally of rich merchants. When services were held in Latin, *illustrations* of Biblical stories on church walls taught the uneducated the lessons of the Bible. The story of Adam, Eve and the apple only required three paintings. For some time it was coincidental that these paintings turned out to be masterpieces. The medium was *not* the message! Later, princes and dukes wanted pictorial records

of their beautiful houses and wives. From Giorgione to Cana-
letto they got them; and were followed in this by the great
merchants.

In the second phase the artist still had need of the patron
but worked independently. Whereas his predecessor had received a commission and occasionally transcended it by producing a masterpiece, *he* 'had something to say'. Haydn wrote
symphonies to please the guests of the Esterhazy family;
Beethoven dedicated his 'Eroica' Symphony to the yet un-
crowned Napoleon because he saw him as a standard-bearer
of freedom. When the Corsican became Emperor, the com-
poser tore up the dedication.

Throughout both phases the artist continued to provide
his contemporaries and their successors with the myths and
symbols that made their lives bearable in a hostile world.
There were always artists who supplied what the majority
needed; and artists who tried to evolve towards heights initially understood by the few. In both cases the artist and his
audience conformed to certain patterns. The worldly char-
acters of, say, Somerset Maugham and James Joyce were
somewhat formed by the need of their respective – and very
different – readers.

In our first phase the artist was mainly a servant, in the
second largely a prophet; though long before artists consciously had 'messages' to transmit, the great among them were
performing both roles simultaneously. R. J. Collingwood gives
us a first-class definition of the word 'prophet' in the way we
are using it here:

> The artist must prophesy, not in the sense that he foretells things
> to come, but in the sense that he tells his audience, at the risk of their
> displeasure, the secrets of their own hearts. . . . The reason why they
> need him is that no community altogether knows its own heart;
> and by failing in the knowledge a community deceives itself on the
> one subject concerning which ignorance means death. For the evils
> which come from that ignorance, the poet as prophet suggests no

remedy, because he has already given one. The remedy is the poem itself. Art is the community medicine for the worst disease of the mind, the corruption of consciousness.[1]

With Collingwood's definition in mind, we turn to the Arts of our own time. If his words are as applicable to us as they were when he wrote them nearly half a century ago, then the outlook is bleak. For Art today is mainly preaching disintegration. The 'happening', something that lasts a few minutes and then disappears for ever, is symbolic of this; so is sculpture made of evaporating materials. Novels are giving way to anti-novels; plays of dialogue to plays of silence; music created by men to music created by electronic devices. Are we to accept this as inevitable and conform to its self-denigrating, dehumanizing principles? Or should we be resisting it strenuously?

INSTANT ART

The situation is further complicated because our attitudes to the Arts are partly fashioned for us. It's not just that people wait to see what the critics say before they buy a book or see a play. It is that newspapers, television and various forms of contrived publicity are constantly attempting to mould our reactions in advance. Instead of being gradually discovered by individuals, a work of art is pronounced a masterpiece before anyone has seen it; then this pronouncement is rammed home with all the pressure of a *Guinness is Good For You* campaign.

The situation may not be black yet, but it is certainly dark grey. *Look Back in Anger* made its way despite an initially lukewarm success, but *Room At The Top* – whatever its merits – was presented as a masterpiece with such rolling of drums and braying of trumpets that failure was nearly impossible. In plays and books, however, the public clings to some standards

[1] R. J. Collingwood, *The Principles of Art*, O.U.P.

of its own because the basic material employed -- words -- is familiar to it in everyday use. If four actors were to stand on a stage and recite the four volumes of the London Telephone Directory simultaneously, most (!) of the public would not be afraid to shout 'nonsense!'. But when we move to the unfamiliar materials used by painters and composers, the public is more vulnerable to overnight discoveries of genius by newspapers and magazines. The sheer strength of the shouts proclaiming the discovery, coupled with a reasonable desire not to look foolish (weren't Beethoven and Stravinsky booed in their days!) leads to tacit acceptance of a great deal of meretricious rubbish.

As with the pressures of fashion, we must constantly be on guard against the discovery of masterpieces. Marshall McLuhan's phrase 'the medium is the message', which we inverted a few pages back, reminds us of the way that thinkers like artists are now presented to us in 'irresistible' package deals. In 1962 Mcluhan, a Canadian professor, published a fascinating book about the effects on Man of the discovery of printing. It was called *The Gutenburg Galaxy*. Two years later he followed it with *Understanding Media*, a book designed to show the effects on Man of the electronic age. Both were received with interest in small, intellectual circles and attempts were made to appraise the value of his original and dramatic theories.

Now, suddenly, in 1967 his work, which is still at the stage where it requires acute, informed analysis, is being foisted on the public by a brilliant publicity campaign. Nor is this campaign one whit less suspect because the professor himself has contributed to it with another, rather spurious book, *The Medium is the Massage*, produced in a gimmicky fashion. Considerable space has been given to Mcluhanism in the Sunday papers and glossy magazines; its founder has been extensively interviewed; and a number of pundits have reacted publicly for or against the movement. As a crowning piece to the campaign, a firm of distinguished educational publishers, aided by Penguin and Sphere Books, have made nearly all the professor's writings available in paperback form, the *mass* publishing medium.

THE SUCCESS TREATMENT

Now the treatment given to Mcluhan is not dissimilar to that meted out to novelists, poets, painters, musicians and sculptors. If our first reaction to the inclusion of creative artists as esoteric as modern poets is one of scepticism, we need only remind ourselves of Dylan Thomas to realize the truth of the matter. There was even a book about Thomas's extended pub-crawl in America; and that book was somehow contrived to augment the legend! From Pop Art to the Theatre of Cruelty, examples abound of the way in which even intellectual arts are presented as the latest 'in' thing – and blithely accepted as such.

We might here pause for long enough to underline that we are not making judgements on the merits of the work of Dylan Thomas, Antonin Artaud or even Marshall Mcluhan. We are only trying to stress that such judgements become increasingly difficult to make under the barrage of publicity put down in their favour; and that such a method of presenting serious art of any sort is dangerous both for the artist and his audience. If Art embodies the myths and legends that Man needs, then to bulldoze him into accepting aspects of it is a real threat to his security.

Art as a fashion or gimmick is the creation of two bodies: the commercial exploiter on the one hand, and newspapers and television on the other. Clearly if a gallery can engender huge advance publicity for a new painter, it can sell his work at high prices. If the campaign is sufficiently well mounted, the attitude to the artist will be fashioned in advance, and lip-service will be widely paid to it. Equally, the newspapers and television are insatiable in their demands for the 'new'. The number of pages in each daily or Sunday paper increases almost annually, while the total amount of *real* news in the world would hardly fill a single page per day. So the papers are left to fall back on features, conjectures, entertainments and gimmicks, and the discovery of new creative artists figures quite high on their lists. True merit becomes almost an ancillary quality.

'The remedy,' wrote Collingwood, 'is the poem itself.' If he is right, then the contemporary artist is painting our (moral) disintegration, our failure to communicate with each other, and our inability to match the progress of the machines we have invented. We can no more afford to turn a blind eye to what the 'poem' says than we can afford to dispense with newspapers because they are mainly filled with 'invented' news.[1] But we must find ways of refusing to conform every time the media of mass communications *tell* us that another genius or masterpiece has been discovered. How can we do this?

DOWN THE KITCHEN SINK

Basically the answer is knowledge. We all know that when a subject being discussed is one in which we are experts, we have no fear of being led astray. Whether it's amateur radio, stamp collecting or pop art, prior mastery of the subject enables us to resist other experts let alone newspaper pseudo-pundits. The snag, though, is that few of us are likely to be expert in more than one field, and almost none of us in the many that daily assault us with their trends, movements and discoveries.

So we have to fall back on an attitude of healthy scepticism. We should train ourselves to be suspicious of any mass promotion, however spontaneous it may seem at first glance.

[1] Those interested should investigate how far this has gone by reading *The Image* by Daniel Boorstin, Penguin.

We should refuse to be swept away by any 'masterpiece' that has been hailed as such long before it has been exposed to the public. *A Legacy*, Sybille Bedford's novel about Germany, which is a work of considerable merit, has gradually built for itself a major reputation despite a quiet, unheralded start. Benjamin Britten's *War Requiem*, on the other hand, was hailed as a work of genius before its first performance. Both still seem major works and so underline the danger of laying down rules about merit. Equally, the so-called 'kitchen sink' novels and plays of the fifties, once welcomed as a tremendous new wave, are now seen by all to have been a comparatively minor by-way of their arts.

Although we may have implied that the main pressures with contemporary arts come from those who gain by manipulation our attitudes to them, we are also subject to influence by friends. If we like and want to keep in with a given circle of people, then it becomes difficult to resist their taste. It is common to find different circles disparaging or raving about different pop-groups, but rarer to find those differences within the circles. This sort of conformity to our friends' taste can be bad, because it means that we are allowing our own sense of judgement to be abrogated by others. Allowing others to decide for us in one area of opinion often leads to similar laziness in others. In the arts we tend to become such passive receivers that the ennobling or transcending experiences of music, painting or literature are dulled for us.

THE VIEW FROM OUTSIDE

Everything we have said about our attitudes to the arts will apply, with qualifications, to all the serious arts; and, with further qualifications, to most of the popular arts. The present tendencies to commercial and mass media exploitation are more dangerous for the serious than for the more popular arts because it is the former which bear the burden of prophecy in

Collingwood's sense. Great art is conceived independently of a mass public; mass art is conceived for it. We have, however, not yet considered a form of art that is vital to urban man, practical as well as aesthetic and influential far beyond the narrow confines of each isolated example. This is architecture.

Narrowly, architecture is the art of designing buildings in which we can live, work and meet. A house that kept out the bad weather and was built to last, a factory that housed machinery and allowed it to function efficiently, a hall that accommodated those using it for a particular purpose would all fill this definition. But these three buildings can rarely be executed in isolation. They have to combine with other houses, factories and halls. Grouped, they are an expression of Man's ability to organize himself into villages and towns. So arranged, they exert an influence on him that can have far-reaching effects on his personal and national character. Anyone doubting this need only remind him or herself of the depressing sight of a slum street or the uplifting effect of a new road like the City of London's Route 11. If we take this a step further and consider the *permanent* effects of the surroundings on a child born in Perugia, Italy, as against one reared in Lewes, England – the latter by no means ugly by English standards – we begin to see how a whole people can be affected by architecture. Not only will the child from Perugia automatically learn a sense of form and colour from the buildings and general townscape around him; he will also be daily uplifted by this beauty and perfection.

Architecture, then, affects us in our day to day living within the buildings where we sleep and work; it also affects us as a group, generation or people by its external forms. It becomes all the more extraordinary to report that students and others, who will protest by the hour about Aldermaston, Vietnam, drugs or the lack of democracy at the London School of Economics, will hardly bother to comment about the hideous – and occasionally beautiful – new buildings that are going to affect them, their children and grandchildren. Those responsible for our new or replacement cities are met with total conformity by those who will have to live in those cities. Let us try to see why this may be as dangerous as our unquestioning acceptance of commercially inspired 'masterpieces'.

EMPTY SHELL

Although we may lack architects of the calibre of America's Mies van der Rohe or Italy's Pier Luigi Nervi, we are not without people of considerable talent. The Smythsons' *Economist* building in St James, Denis Lasdun's flats near by or Ronald Ward's Vickers Tower are three modern examples that are evidence of this. Yet the majority of post-war building is much more like the huge, absolutely uninspired Shell block that dominates the Festival Hall end of Waterloo Bridge. One of the main reasons for this is that much of the money for post-war building has come from the major insurance companies. As they have provided the funds, so their controlling boards have had a say in design. Most of these boards consist of men in their sixties, men whose tastes (if any!) were formed in the arid architectural deserts immediately before the Second World War.

What is even worse is that where these men have not actually imposed a veto on the new, exciting or experimental, architects have been afraid that they may do and have produced duller and more conservative designs. The result of all this is that the post-war rebuilding of England has been singularly uninspired. In a period where the eleven-plus or an extra 'O' level has been a matter of life or death, a whole generation has been allowed to grow up without any education in the appreciation of architecture. Ignorance has ensured the conformity that property developers and insurance companies have needed to net the maximum profitability per square foot. Such visions as the Abercrombie plan for the development of the area around St Paul's have remained visions pure and simple.

The willingness to join every trend in the latest painting, sculptural or musical fashion contrasts strikingly with our failure to care about contemporary architecture. It has come about because we can appear to divorce ourselves from the fine arts and so are willing to experiment; we have to live with architecture and so play safe. Yet our lack of concern over the buildings, streets and towns that are being put up in our name at our expense is a folly that generations will have to pay for. The LCC (as it was) housing and shopping development at Roehampton is a straightforward, reasonably priced example of what can be done to ensure that people live in friendly, landscaped, well-proportioned buildings. In the same way, the GLC, and County Councils like Leicester and Hereford, have shown what can be achieved in school building for the same cost as the dull, stodgy edifices that are to be found all over Surrey. Children are affected by the quality of the buildings in which they receive their education. Conformity to the second rate by lack of interest in what is being done in our name has lost us opportunities that may never recur.

DISCUSSION POINTS

1. Does Man *need* Art whatever the level of his sophistication or education?

2. Should he protest against whatever he considers false or gimmicky, remembering how often contemporary audiences have been wrong in the past?

3. Do buildings and cities help form the character of those who live in them?

4. And, if the answer to 3 is 'yes', how can we refuse to conform to the architecture imposed on us?

9: WHY CONFORM?

There have always been full-time rebels against established society. We need look no further than Jesus for someone who renounced all the values of the society in which he lived, then sought in their place to promote purer ones. Nearer our own times we have the bohemians and expatriates of the twenties, though theirs was a selfish rebellion: they were not seeking to put society right; only to leave it. After the Second World War came the beatniks, a group of wanderers, tramp-style, emerging from the writers and poets of San Francisco. Now we have hippies and flower people. The message is constant: opt out of current society.

Initially it is easy to be sympathetic to this attitude. After all, we may concur, politicians *are* largely cynical, bent mainly on improving their personal reputations. Power corrupts even the few genuine idealists among them. Western society is ruled by the profit motive, and, Marks and Spencer's and the John Lewis Partnership notwithstanding, a pretty grimy, scrdid motive it is. Proletarian man, freed at last from the grind of near-poverty, has shown that his wants are little different from his capitalist bosses: a fridge, a telly and a car. What incentive is there for a decent teenager to join this mob?

But almost before the sympathy starts to declare itself, two snags appear. Firstly no state of society has ever been peacefully reformed by fleeing from it. Democratic change can only come from within, and the more people demand that change the likelier it is to come. If enough people put care of the elderly before new bingo halls; butter before guns; and beautiful cities before rosy balance sheets, we are more likely to attain higher standards than if they just turn their backs on the whole thing.

Secondly, even those who want to opt out only want to avoid the responsibilities and duties. Although they refuse to vote or play the profit game, they still want to use the buses that society runs, the same society that is run by politicians and company directors. Similarly they still want to get medical attention when ill, still want to buy food in shops, to use electricity and gas – still want to live on what society provides. As long as only a tiny minority wants to opt out, the possibility exists. The moment the numbers begin to increase, society is threatened with breakdown.

If we revert for a moment to the motoring example used earlier in this book, the position becomes clearer. With half a dozen cars in the whole of England, road rules would hardly be necessary. With six million vehicles chaos would be instantaneous without them. A few people can still opt to take their cars off the roads into fields, but even then there will have to be rules when enough of them follow suit. And the only way between fields is by the existing road networks where they would be forced into contact with millions of other cars. Opting out is a dream, as pleasant to contemplate as any other sort of utopia – and as impractical.

THE NEED FOR POLITICS

Once we realize this, then we realize that refusal to involve ourselves in the making of traffic laws means accepting those made for us, however unpleasant. The Highway Code lays down traffic rules; politics govern the laws that make it possible for millions of people to live with minimal friction in close proximity to each other. We can be as nonconforming as we like *within* the political spectrum, but to conform in the sense of casting a vote or supporting a party means retaining a fractional but finally important say in electing the legislature. It is useless to bemoan the election of a Tory (or Labour) M.P. by a handful of votes in a given constituency if we and our friends failed to cast the dozen votes that might have changed the result. Government is essential. Good government is more likely where *all* the governed exercise the choosing of their leaders.

When we move from the larger unit of the country to the smaller one like the office, works or family, most of the same rules apply. None of these units can function efficiently unless everyone is contributing as well as drawing benefit. But if we are to conform to *reasonable* demands by fathers and bosses, then we have every right to expect our situations or needs to be taken into account. It may seem a denial of liberty when the departmental manager tells us to get our hair cut, but while we are working for a firm, the image we project becomes part of the firm's image. A badly dressed or dirty employee might lose the firm an order or contract. But if we accede this much, then we have every right to consideration in our turn. We should not expect to have to conform to rules whose justification is not explained to us; nor to work doubly hard on projects whose aim has not yet been made clear. If our conformity or co-operation is required for the good of the organization, so is that of our seniors.

The readiness to give as well as take applies as much in the home as in the office. Frequently we hear parents berating their children for selfishness or refusal to make small sacrifices. Yet those same parents are unwilling in their turn to put the children first some of the time. Nor must we lose sight of the fact that it is biologically necessary for children to break away from their parents. However much they understand the need for this, most parents will put up some sort of rear-guard action against it. Nonconformity to the standards laid down or implied by the parent is one of the many ways of rebelling against this rear-guard action.

CONFORMING TO REBELLION

Most of the points at issue between young people and their parents, like refusing to have their hair cut or coming in very late or dressing in flamboyant clothes, are very small and, in themselves, quite unimportant. Many boys with excessively long hair or girls with excessively short skirts may look aesthetically unpleasing, but rarely enough to invoke the passionate opposition that older relations exhibit. They are, of course, symbolic of the announcement by the young of their struggle for independence. From our point of view in considering reasonable standards of conduct, they are not vital. As long as people are clean and not yet representing organizations which may be harmed by their eccentricities, it is difficult to see what all the fuss is about. Except – if there was no fuss at all, then the same people would start looking for other ways of proclaiming their new-found independence!

Mention of hair and clothes style reminds us of fashions. We live in a capitalist, consumer society where ever greater sales are the key to economic success. This in turn means that manufacturers are anxious for consumers not only to use their products, but to use them out or use them up as well. Constant replacement increases the volume of the market. This can be artificially aided by accenting new fashions or trends to make the consumer feel that what he possesses is already out of date.

One of the factors of post-war sociological changes is the emergence of the financially independent teenager. Considerable efforts have been made by manufacturers and advertising agents to stimulate this sector of demand. In its train has come an unprecedented accent on youth, which has quickly spread from the young themselves to kidding the middle-aged and even older that they are as young as ever! In such an atmosphere it is easy to convince people that whatever they bought a year or five years ago is out of date. Fashion leads the way.

This is not entirely bad, since it is in our interests for consumption to be high once we accept the capitalist, consumer society. But the excessive attention paid to fashion has carried things too far. Waste is rife because of it; individuality is threatened because of it. As with so many other aspects of life, balance is needed. It is manifestly ridiculous to throw away good articles because they are 'out of fashion'. It is as stupid to wear an unsuitable garment or hair style because it is 'in fashion'. The strength of the fashion-makers is great, since they have so much to gain from success. We would be wise, therefore, to cultivate a built-in resistance to fashion. Even so, some of it will still get through. At least the more extreme examples may be avoided.

THEN WHAT?

Almost everything I have considered has produced a response that is mainly negative. Don't expect something for nothing – those opting out do; don't evade the responsibilities that are automatically ours by being part of modern, highly complex society; don't be swept away by trends and fashions to the point of becoming stupid or wasteful; don't cultivate nonconformity for its own sake. Isn't it possible, though, to make some more positive suggestions for a moral code? Didn't I suggest, earlier in this book, that we must find something to replace the Christian ethic by which Man has lived for the last 2,000 years?

I did, and, in the bigger sense, we must. But it would be presumptuous for a short book inquiring into some of our current moral situations to pretend that it could offer the answers that have been eluding thinkers and churchmen for the last twenty or thirty years. The whole edifice of Christian morality, much of which is still there for believers and agnostics alike, will take years to replace. Meanwhile, though, we need some form of rough rule of thumb by which to live.

Some contributory attitudes have been suggested as we have looked at various aspects of the current scene. At the centre of everything, however, is our attitude to each other. Our behaviour to friends, neighbours, lovers or just fellow citizens is a key feature of our lives. And here, perhaps, a fairly simple rule *can* be stated: we must *always* regard other people as ends in themselves; *never* as a means to our own ends. This automatically condemns murder, stealing, sexual exploitation and a host of other actions where we are only using people to further our own ends. But it is also a fair guide to many smaller, everyday problems.

It's not as easy as it may sound in a simple statement. Moral problems are rarely uncomplicated. Stealing from a man is wrong because it means *using* him for your own ends. But stealing from a very rich man, who won't help, to save a starving peasant? Can that be immoral? So that even if our rule of reasonable conduct is wise, it will inevitably have many, many exceptions.

Conformity is never a clear, cut-and-dried attitude, not least because standards are always changing. It is always a balance between the mainly right and the slightly wrong. We may feel that on balance pre-marital sexual intercourse is not advisable, but there will still be cases where it would be wrong to forbid it. Or we may feel that on balance it should be permitted, and there would still be individuals for whom such freedom would be dangerous. Human beings may be similar to one another; they are almost never identical.

Why conform? Simply because society is so numerous and complex that there would be chaos if most of us refused to most of the time. Why refuse to conform on occasion? Because the whole trend of modern society is towards homogeneity, towards the uniform common man. Somehow we must find a balance between the two, a difficult and infinitely exciting task.